THE COMPLETE
PASTRY COOK

THE COMPLETE
PASTRY COOK

Carol Bowen

CENTURY PUBLISHING
LONDON

For Peter, whose appreciation of fine food has always been an inspiration to me.

Copyright © Carol Bowen 1983

All rights reserved

First published in Great Britain in 1983
by Century Publishing Co. Ltd,
76 Old Compton Street, London W1V 5PA

British Library Cataloguing in Publication Data

Bowen, Carol
  The complete pastry cook.
  1. Pastry
  I. Title
  641.8′65   TX773

ISBN 0-7126-0256-9

Designed by Patrick McLeavey & Sue Storey
Illustrated by Lily Whitlock

Printed in Great Britain in 1983 by
Richard Clay (The Chaucer Press) Ltd, Bungay, Suffolk

CONTENTS

INTRODUCTION

The making of pastry in England dates back to Saxon and Norman times, when a flour and water paste, called a huff paste, was wrapped around a precious piece of meat to keep in the juices while baking. The resultant inedible crust was then discarded before serving. By the Middle Ages, fat and spices were added to the paste, making it easier to work with principally, but also adding flavour. In time the pastry was eaten as a delicacy since it gradually became recognised that the juices seeped into the crust and produced a delicious dish in its own right.

Filled pies became more and more popular and soon earned their place as the most popular centre piece at many a court banquet. They were often the focus of amusement, for they were often filled with live birds or frogs and even dwarfs!

Needless to say, almost every country and civilisation makes its claim to the origins of pastry - early records show that the Chinese and Greeks also had early forms of what could be called a basic pastry. Whatever the answer, the development of pastry from those early days has been somewhat remarkable.

Today we have recipes for pastry ranging from the simple shortcrust to the more complicated puff. Recipes are also being constantly developed with the introduction of appliances that make pastry making easier.

It isn't just the British that stake their culinary reputation on a pastry speciality, like a raised pie, apple pie, steamed pudding or delicious roly-poly. The French compete admirably with their pastries en croûte, fruit layered tarts and savoury quiches, and the Greeks provide yet more variety with baklavas and savoury nibbles made from phyllo pastry.

There is undeniably an art to pastry making but one that is simple to learn. The basic ingredients hold part of the key to success - recognise each of their roles and you can't go far wrong. Study the basic recipes and the procedures for making pastry dishes and all will become clear.

The 'Complete Pastry Cook' has been compiled with these aims in mind - it is also hoped that it encompasses almost every type of pastry known as well as some delicious ideas for pastry dishes.

Pastry dishes have quickly become universal favourites and almost everyone, as a result, has a family favourite - and thankfully want to share it. Many thanks go to all those colleagues and friends who shared their recipes but especially to my sister Jackie whose relentless testing, tasting and help continued to inspire me.

CAROL BOWEN

BASIC INGREDIENTS

Give any two people the same ingredients and recipe and they may produce two different pastries - it is all a matter of handling. If you give the same two the choice of type of flour, fat and liquid for their recipe they will *undoubtedly* produce two different pastries. Different flours, fats, liquids, enrichening and raising agents will behave in different ways and not only produce differences in texture but also in flavour and colour. Even the temperatures of the ingredients used will play their part in the pastry end result.

FLOURS
In almost all cases plain flour is recommended for pastry making. The exceptions are suet crust pastry and phyllo or strudel pastry. Strudel or phyllo pastry needs a strong plain flour where there is extra gluten and suet crust pastry needs a self-raising flour or plain flour with a raising agent for its light texture. Wherever plain flour is used you can experiment by using wholemeal or wholewheat flour - this is particularly successful with shortcrust and hot water crust pastries. (After sifting brown flours, always tip back the sieve contents into the flour.)

FATS
Butter, lard and margarines are the most popular fats used in pastry making but you can use a proprietary blend of vegetable shortenings especially developed for pastry making (follow the packet instructions for best results). Lard in a shortcrust type of pastry gives the flakiness required and butter or margarine the firmness, flavour and colour often liked. For these reasons a mixture of lard and margarine or butter is recommended. Use fats that are firm or lightly chilled for rubbing in - fat that is too hard can be difficult to rub in and can produce a blistered end result to the pastry.

LIQUIDS
Water, fruit juices or eggs are often the liquids used to bind pastry dry ingredients together. Generally a chilled or iced water is recommended. Only add just the amount the pastry needs to bind loosely together - adding too much water will produce a hard tough pastry.

SEASONINGS

Salt, sugar, spices and other seasonings can all be used with success in making pastry. Add just the amounts recommended in the basic recipes for good results. The flavourings are generally best added with the dry ingredients and sifted in wherever possible to achieve a good overall blending of flavours.

SUET

For the recipes in this book, shop bought suet has been used. You can however achieve excellent results with fresh suet. Always shred fresh suet before use.

RAISING AGENTS

Baking powder and eggs are the favourite raising agents in pastries, although steam is the raising agent in puff, flaky and rough puff pastries. To achieve light-as-air results, dampen rather than grease the baking tray for such pastries. In choux pastry the raising agents are both eggs and steam.

BASIC PASTRY RECIPES

Shortcrust Pastry

Everyone seems to have their favourite recipe for this versatile and widely used pastry and this is mine. I prefer to use a mixture of lard and butter as the fat since the lard provides the light texture I like and butter the unbeatable flavour. You can however, use all butter, all lard, all margarine or almost any mixture according to taste and availability.

Although simple to make, the essential ingredients for successful shortcrust pastry are often not the basic ingredients themselves – but a cool surface, a light touch and careful handling. The tips below should help you achieve a pastry to be proud of:

★ Make sure all the ingredients, the surface and mixing utensils are cold or even chilled before use
★ Measure ingredients accurately – too much or too little of any ingredient can spell disaster
★ Rub in the fat lightly with just the fingertips – avoid the palms of the hands which quickly become warm
★ Lift the dry ingredients high to incorporate as much air as possible so producing a light pastry
   Allow the pastry to 'rest' in the refrigerator for 15–30
★ minutes before rolling out. The pastry is less likely to shrink on baking if this is observed
★ Knead and roll out quickly and lightly taking care not to over handle the dough or to stretch it unduly

Makes 1 (20-23-cm/8-9-inch) flan, 12 double-crust tartlets, 4 small savoury pies or 1 large pie crust

225g (8 oz) plain flour   *50g (2 oz) lard*
¼ teaspoon salt   *2-3 tablespoons iced water*
50g (2 oz) butter

Sift the flour and salt into a mixing bowl. Cut the butter and lard into small pieces and toss in the flour lightly. Rub the fats into the flour with the fingertips until the mixture resembles fine breadcrumbs.

Add the water, sprinkling it over the rubbed-in mixture and bind with a round-bladed knife and then the fingertips to a firm but pliable dough.

Turn onto a lightly-floured surface and knead lightly until smooth and free from cracks. Roll out thinly on a lightly-floured surface and cook in a preheated moderately hot oven (200°C, 400°F, Gas Mark 6) until lightly-browned, or according to specific recipe instructions.

VARIATIONS

Wholemeal shortcrust pastry: Prepare and cook as above but use wholemeal flour instead of plain.

Nut shortcrust pastry: Prepare and cook as above but add 25g (1 oz) chopped nuts of your choice with the water. Take care not to over handle this pastry. Walnuts, almonds, hazelnuts, cashew nuts and Brazil nuts are all suitable. If using salted peanuts then do not use any salt in the basic recipe.

Orange shortcrust pastry: Prepare and cook as above but add the finely grated rind of ½ small orange to the rubbed-in ingredients before adding the water.

Lemon shortcrust pastry: Prepare and cook as above but add the finely grated rind of ½ lemon to the rubbed-in ingredients before adding the water.

Cinnamon shortcrust pastry: Prepare and cook as above but sift the flour and salt with 1 teaspoon ground cinnamon.

Spicy shortcrust pastry: Prepare and cook as above but sift the flour and salt with 1 teaspoon ground mixed spice.

Curry shortcrust pastry: Prepare and cook as above but sift the flour and salt with 1-2 teaspoons curry powder (strength and amount according to taste).

Herby shortcrust pastry: Prepare and cook as above but add 1½-2 teaspoons dried herbs of your choice to the rubbed-in ingredients before adding the water.

Ginger shortcrust pastry: Prepare and cook as above but sift the flour and salt with 1 teaspoon ground ginger. Stir in 15g (½ oz) very finely chopped stem ginger before adding the water if a strong ginger flavour is liked.

Turmeric shortcrust pastry: Prepare and cook as above but sift the flour with 1-2 teaspoons turmeric.

FREEZING

Baked or unbaked shortcrust pastry can be frozen for up to 6 months.

Quick Mix Shortcrust Pastry

This is the quickest pastry that I know you can make by hand. It uses soft-blend tub margarine which is blended with a little flour and water to form a smooth paste. The remaining flour is then incorporated to make a smooth dough.

Makes 1 (20-cm/8-inch) flan

100g (4 oz) soft-blend tub
  margarine
175g (6 oz) plain flour

1 tablespoon iced water
¼ teaspoon salt

Place the margarine, 2 tablespoons of the flour and the water in a bowl. Cream for about 30 seconds until light and fluffy. Sift the remaining flour with the salt and add to the creamed mixture, mixing lightly to form a fairly soft dough.

Turn onto a lightly-floured surface and knead until smooth and free from cracks. Roll out thinly on a lightly-floured surface and cook in a preheated moderately hot oven (190°C, 375°F, Gas Mark 5) until lightly-browned, or according to specific recipe instructions.

Shortcrust Blender Pastry

Blenders are marvellous pieces of equipment for making pastry. So much so, it is worth making quantities in bulk to store in the refrigerator or freezer. This shortcrust pastry recipe is ideal for general use but follow the richer variation for sweet pies, flans and continental specialities.

Makes 1 (20-cm/8-inch) flan, 12 double-crust tartlets, 4 small savoury pies, 4 small Cornish pasties, 1 large pie crust

225g (8 oz) plain flour
¼ teaspoon salt

100g (4 oz) butter
2 tablespoons iced water

Place the flour, salt and butter, cut into small pieces, in the blender goblet or bowl. Mix on the lowest speed, increasing to medium speed, until the mixture resembles fine breadcrumbs, about 30–60 seconds. Add the water and mix on the lowest speed until the ingredients just bind together.

Turn onto a lightly-floured surface and knead lightly until smooth and free from cracks. Wrap in polythene or cling film and chill for 15 minutes.

Roll out thinly on a lightly-floured surface and cook in a preheated moderately hot oven (200°C, 400°F, Gas Mark 6) until lightly-browned, or according to specific recipe instructions.

VARIATIONS

Wholemeal blender pastry: Prepare and cook as above but use wholemeal flour instead of plain flour.

Cheese blender pastry: Prepare and cook as above but add ½ teaspoon dry mustard powder with the flour and salt and add 75g (3 oz) grated Cheddar cheese with the water.

Rich shortcrust blender pastry: Place 175g (6 oz) flour, 75g (3 oz) diced butter and 25g (1 oz) castor sugar in the blender goblet or bowl. Mix on the lowest speed until the mixture resembles fine breadcrumbs, about 30–60 seconds. Add 1 egg yolk and 1 tablespoon iced water and mix on the lowest speed until the ingredients just bind together.

FREEZING

Freeze baked or unbaked blender pastries in the freezer for up to 6 months.

Oatmeal Shortcrust Pastry

Makes 1 (20-cm/8-inch) flan or 1 medium pie crust

100g (4 oz) plain flour
100g (4 oz) fine oatmeal
pinch of salt

50g (2 oz) butter or lard
water to bind

Mix the flour, oatmeal and salt in a mixing bowl. Cut the butter or lard into small pieces and toss in the oatmeal mixture. Rub in with the fingertips until the mixture resembles fine breadcrumbs. Add sufficient water to bind to a firm but pliable dough.

Turn onto a lightly-floured surface and knead until smooth and free from cracks. Wrap in polythene or cling film and chill for 15 minutes before use.

Roll out on a lightly-floured surface and cook in a preheated moderately hot oven (200°C, 400°F, Gas Mark 6) until lightly browned and cooked, or according to specific recipe instructions.

Basic Cheese Pastry

Makes 1 (23-cm/9-inch) flan, 12–14 tartlets, 1 large pie crust or 12–14 pastry boats

225g (8 oz) plain flour
½ teaspoon salt
¼ teaspoon freshly ground
  pepper
½ teaspoon dry mustard
  powder
pinch of cayenne pepper

50g (2 oz) butter or margarine
50g (2 oz) lard
40g (1½ oz) mature Cheddar
  cheese, grated
3 teaspoons grated Parmesan
  cheese
4 tablespoons cold water

Sift the flour, salt, pepper, mustard powder and cayenne pepper into a mixing bowl. Cut the butter or margarine and lard into small pieces and rub into the flour with the fingertips until the mixture resembles fine breadcrumbs. Stir in the Cheddar and Parmesan, mixing well. Add the water and bind to a firm but manageable dough.

Turn onto a lightly-floured surface and knead lightly until smooth and free from cracks. Wrap in polythene or cling film and chill for 15–20 minutes before using.

Roll out on a lightly-floured surface and cook in a preheated moderately hot oven (200°C, 400°F, Gas Mark 6) or according to the specific recipe instructions.

Cream Cheese Pastry

Makes 10 tartlets, 1 (20-cm/8-inch) flan or 10 pastry boats

75g (3 oz) full-fat cream cheese
75g (3 oz) butter
1 tablespoon single cream

¼ teaspoon salt
200g (7 oz) plain flour
25g (1 oz) cornflour

Cream the cheese with the butter, single cream and salt until light and fluffy. Sift the flour with the cornflour and add to the creamed mixture. Mix to a fairly soft dough with a round-bladed knife.

Turn onto a lightly-floured surface and knead lightly until smooth and free from cracks. Wrap in polythene or cling film and chill for 30 minutes before using.

Roll out thinly on a lightly-floured surface and cook in a preheated moderately hot oven (190°C, 375°F, Gas Mark 5) or according to specific recipe instructions.

Wheatgerm Pastry

Makes 1 (23-cm/9-inch) shallow plate pie, 1 medium pie crust or 1 (20-cm/8-inch) flan

125g (4½ oz) wholemeal flour
65g (2½ oz) wheatgerm
pinch of salt

100g (4 oz) butter or margarine
3 tablespoons iced water

Mix the flour, wheatgerm and salt in a mixing bowl. Cut the butter into small pieces and toss lightly in the flour mixture. Rub in the butter with the fingertips until the mixture resembles fine breadcrumbs. Add the water and mix, with a round-bladed knife, to a firm but pliable dough.

Turn onto a lightly-floured surface until smooth and free from cracks. Wrap in polythene or cling film and chill for 30 minutes before using.

Roll out on a lightly-floured surface and cook in a preheated moderately hot oven (200°C, 400°F, Gas Mark 6) until lightly brown and cooked, or according to specific recipe instructions.

Soured Cream Pastry

Makes 1 (23-cm/9-inch) shallow plate pie or 1 medium pie crust

175g (6 oz) plain flour
100g (4 oz) butter

7 tablespoons soured cream

Sift the flour into a mixing bowl. Cut the butter into small pieces and rub into the flour with the fingertips until the mixture resembles fine breadcrumbs. Add the soured cream and mix, with a round-bladed knife, to a firm but pliable dough.

Turn onto a lightly-floured surface and knead lightly until smooth and free from cracks. Wrap in polythene or cling film and chill for 30 minutes before using.

Roll out on a lightly-floured surface and cook in a preheated moderately hot oven (190°C, 375°F, Gas Mark 5) until lightly browned, or according to specific recipe instructions.

Nutmeg Pastry

Makes 8–10 tartlets, 1 (20-cm/8-inch) flan, 10 pastry boats or 1 medium pie crust

175g (6 oz) plain flour
1 teaspoon ground nutmeg
pinch of salt

75g (3 oz) butter or margarine
1–2 tablespoons water

Sift the flour, nutmeg and salt into a mixing bowl. Cut the butter or margarine into small pieces and rub into the flour with the fingertips until the mixture resembles fine breadcrumbs. Add the water and mix to a firm but manageable dough.

Turn onto a lightly-floured surface and knead lightly until smooth and free from cracks. Use as required. Roll out on a lightly-floured surface and cook in a preheated moderately hot oven (190°C, 375°F, Gas Mark 5) or according to specific recipe instructions.

Sweet Coffee Pastry

Makes 1 (20-cm/8-inch) flan or 1 large pie crust

225g (8 oz) plain flour less 1 tablespoon
2–3 teaspoons instant coffee powder (according to taste)
50g (2 oz) butter

50g (2 oz) lard
2 teaspoons brown sugar
2–3 tablespoons iced water or milk

Sift the flour and coffee powder into a mixing bowl. Cut the butter and lard into small pieces and toss in the flour lightly. Rub the fats into the flour with the fingertips until the mixture resembles fine breadcrumbs.

Add the sugar and mix well. Add the water, sprinkling it over the rubbed-in mixture, and bind with a round-bladed knife and then the fingertips to a firm but pliable dough.

Turn onto a lightly-floured surface and knead until smooth and free from cracks. Roll out thinly on a lightly-floured surface and cook in a preheated moderately hot oven (200°C, 400°F, Gas Mark 6) until cooked, or according to specific recipe instructions.

FREEZING
As shortcrust pastry.

Sweet Chocolate Pastry

Makes 1 (20-cm/8-inch) flan or 1 large pie crust

225g (8 oz) plain flour less
  1 tablespoon
1 tablespoon cocoa powder
50g (2 oz) butter

50g (2 oz) lard
2 teaspoons castor sugar
2–3 tablespoons iced water or
  milk

Sift the flour and cocoa powder into a mixing bowl. Cut the butter and lard into small pieces and toss in the flour lightly. Rub the fats into the flour with the fingertips until the mixture resembles fine breadcrumbs.

Add the sugar and mix well. Add the water, sprinkling it over the rubbed-in mixture, and bind with a round-bladed knife and then the fingertips to a firm but pliable dough.

Turn onto a lightly-floured surface and knead until smooth and free from cracks. Roll out thinly on a lightly-floured surface and cook in a preheated moderately hot oven (200°C, 400°F, Gas Mark 6) until cooked, or according to specific recipe instructions.

FREEZING
As shortcrust pastry.

Peanut Butter Pastry

Makes 4 pasties, 1 (23-cm/9-inch) deep flan or 12 tartlets

225g (8 oz) self-raising flour
¼ teaspoon salt
25g (1 oz) butter or margarine

100g (4 oz) smooth peanut
  butter
1–2 tablespoons water

Sift the flour and salt into a mixing bowl. Rub the butter and peanut butter into the flour with the fingertips until the mixture resembles fine breadcrumbs. Add the water and bind to a firm but manageable dough. Wrap in polythene or cling film and chill for 15–20 minutes before using.

Roll out on a lightly-floured surface and cook in a preheated moderately hot oven (200°C, 400°F, Gas Mark 6) or according to specific recipe instructions.

VARIATION
Sweet peanut butter pastry: Prepare as above but add 25g (1 oz) castor sugar after rubbing in the butter and peanut butter.

19

Onion Pastry

Makes 1 (20-cm/8-inch) flan, 4 small savoury pies or 1 large pie crust

225g (8 oz) plain flour
50g (2 oz) butter
50g (2 oz) lard
½ small onion, peeled, chopped

and cooked in a little butter
then cooled
½ teaspoon onion powder
2–3 tablespoons iced water

Sift the flour into a mixing bowl. Cut the butter and lard into small pieces and toss in the flour lightly. Rub the fats into the flour with the fingertips until the mixture resembles fine breadcrumbs.

Add the onion and onion powder, mixing well to blend. Add the water, sprinkling it over the rubbed-in mixture, and bind with a round-bladed knife and then the fingertips to a firm but pliable dough.

Turn onto a lightly-floured surface and knead lightly until smooth and free from cracks. Roll out thinly on a lightly-floured surface and cook in a preheated moderately hot oven (200°C, 400°F, Gas Mark 6) until lightly-browned, or according to specific recipe instructions.

FREEZING
As for shortcrust pastry.

Bacon Pastry

Makes 1 (20-cm/8-inch) flan or 4 small savoury pastries

225g (8 oz) plain flour
50g (2 oz) butter
50g (2 oz) lard
2 rashers back bacon, rinds

removed, cooked and
crumbled finely
2–3 tablespoons iced water

Sift the flour into a mixing bowl. Cut the butter and lard into small pieces and toss in the flour lightly. Rub the fats into the flour with the fingertips until the mixture resembles fine breadcrumbs.

Add the bacon and mix well to blend. Add the water, sprinkling it over the rubbed-in mixture, and bind with a round-bladed knife and then the fingertips to a firm but pliable dough.

Turn onto a lightly-floured surface and knead lightly until smooth and free from cracks. Roll out thinly on a lightly-floured surface and cook in a preheated moderately hot oven (200°C, 400°F, Gas Mark 6) until lightly-browned, or according to specific recipe instructions.

FREEZING
Freeze baked or unbaked for up to 3 months.

Coconut Pastry

Makes 1 (20-cm/8-inch) flan or 12 double-crust tartlets

200g (7 oz) plain flour
25g (1 oz) desiccated coconut
50g (2 oz) butter
50g (2 oz) lard

1-2 teaspoons castor sugar
(optional)
2-3 tablespoons iced water

Sift the flour into a mixing bowl and stir in the coconut. Cut the butter and lard into small pieces and toss in the flour mixture lightly. Rub the fats into the flour with the fingertips until the mixture resembles fine breadcrumbs.

Add the sugar if used, mixing well. Add the water, sprinkling it over the rubbed-in mixture, and bind with a round-bladed knife and then the fingertips to a firm but pliable dough.

Turn onto a lightly-floured surface and knead lightly until smooth and free from cracks. Roll out thinly on a lightly-floured surface and cook in a preheated moderately hot oven (200°C, 400°F, Gas Mark 6) until lightly-browned, or according to specific recipe instructions.

FREEZING
Freeze baked or unbaked for up to 4 months.

Pâte Sucrée

Pâte sucrée, better known as French flan pastry, is a very rich but light pastry made from flour, sugar, butter and eggs. The secret of the golden brown, crisp, biscuit-like texture lies in the special preparation of the dough. The method of mixing is called the 'well' method since it involves placing the butter, sugar and eggs in a well in the flour prior to mixing. The result is a pastry that is excellent for use in preparing sweet flans, pastries and continental specialities.

Makes 1 (20-cm/8-inch) flan, 12 tartlets or 12–14 pastry boats

175g (6 oz) plain flour
pinch of salt
75g (3 oz) castor sugar

75g (3 oz) butter, softened
2 large (size 1, 2) egg yolks
2-3 drops vanilla essence

Sift the flour and salt onto a cool work surface. Make a well in the centre. Place the sugar in the well with the butter, cut into small pieces, egg yolks and vanilla essence. Gradually draw the flour into the well with the fingertips of one hand, pinching to bind the dough together.

Turn onto a lightly-floured surface and knead lightly until smooth and free from cracks. Wrap in polythene or cling film and chill for 1 hour before using.

Roll out thinly on a lightly-floured surface and cook in a preheated moderately hot oven (190°C, 375°F, Gas Mark 5), or according to specific recipe instructions.

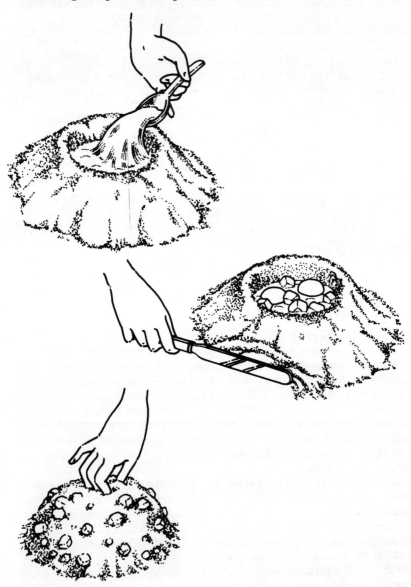

Galette Pastry

Makes about 10 (7.5-cm/3-inch) galettes

225g (8 oz) plain flour
25g (1 oz) icing sugar
150g (5 oz) butter, softened

2 small (size 6) egg yolks
2 drops vanilla essence

Sift the flour and icing sugar onto a cool work surface. Make a well in the centre. Place the butter, cut into small pieces, egg yolks and vanilla essence in the well. Gradually draw the flour mixture into the well with the fingertips of one hand, pinching to bind the dough together.

Turn onto a lightly-floured surface and knead lightly until smooth and free from cracks. Wrap in polythene or cling film and chill for about 1 hour before using.

Roll out thinly on a lightly-floured surface and use to line galette tins. Cook in a preheated moderately hot oven (190°C, 375°F, Gas Mark 5) until lightly browned, or according to specific recipe instructions.

Traditionally galettes are baked 'blind' and then cooled. Fill with soft summer fruits, fruit purées, confectioner's custard or glacé fruits as liked. Glaze if liked.

Sweet Flan Pastry

This is a rich pastry suitable for sweet flans. It is made in much the same way as shortcrust pastry. To use this pastry for savoury flans simply omit the sugar.

Makes 1 (20-cm/8-inch) flan

175g (6 oz) plain flour
pinch of salt
75g (3 oz) butter

40g (1½ oz) lard
1½ teaspoons castor sugar
1 large (size 1, 2) egg, beaten

Sift the flour and salt into a mixing bowl. Cut the butter and lard into small pieces and toss lightly in the flour. Rub the fats into the flour with the fingertips until the mixture resembles fine breadcrumbs.

Add the sugar and toss well to blend. Add the egg and mix with a round-bladed knife and the fingertips to a firm but pliable dough.

Turn onto a lightly-floured surface and knead lightly until smooth and free from cracks. Roll out thinly on a lightly-floured surface and cook in a preheated moderately hot oven (200°C, 400°F, Gas Mark 6) until lightly-browned, or according to specific recipe instructions.

Almond Pastry

Makes 10-12 tartlets, 1 (20-cm/8-inch) flan or 10-12 pastry boats

175g (6 oz) plain flour
¼ teaspoon salt
75g (3 oz) ground almonds
100g (4 oz) butter or margarine

75g (3 oz) castor sugar
1 large (size 1, 2) egg, beaten
2-3 drops almond essence
(optional)

Sift the flour and salt into a mixing bowl. Add the almonds and mix well to blend. Place the butter, castor sugar, egg and almond essence, if using, in the centre of the dry ingredients and work with the fingertips of one hand, gradually drawing the dry ingredients into the mixture to form a fairly soft dough.

Turn out onto a lightly-floured surface and knead lightly until smooth and free from cracks. Wrap in polythene or cling film and chill for 1 hour before using.

Roll out thinly on a lightly-floured surface and cook in a preheated moderately hot oven (190°C, 375°F, Gas Mark 5) or according to specific recipe instructions.

Walnut Pastry

Makes 12-14 tartlets, 1 (20-cm/8-inch) double-crust pie or 12-14 pastry boats

225g (8 oz) plain flour
50g (2 oz) walnuts, finely
   chopped
100g (4 oz) butter, softened

75g (3 oz) castor sugar
2 egg yolks
2 tablespoons water

Sift the flour onto a clean, dry work surface and sprinkle over the chopped walnuts. Make a well in the centre. Place the butter, cut into small pieces, sugar, egg yolks and water in the well. Work with the fingertips of one hand, gradually drawing the dry ingredients into the mixture to form a fairly soft but manageable dough.

Knead lightly until smooth and free from cracks. Wrap in polythene or cling film and chill for 30 minutes before using.

Roll out thinly on a lightly-floured surface and cook in a preheated moderately hot oven (190°C, 375°F, Gas Mark 5) or according to specific recipe instructions.

Puff Pastry

Puff pastry is perhaps one of the most complicated pastries to make – not because the recipe or method is complicated but because it needs careful handling, a light touch and that essential but expensive ingredient, time. The results however are so rewarding that devotees of home-made puff pastry raise their hands in horror at the shop bought variety. I confess to using both, although would opt for the former if only time would allow. Perhaps the simplest solution is to make puff pastry in bulk since it stores so well in both refrigerator and freezer. The recipe below makes a large quantity.

Puff pastry is undoubtedly the richest of pastries since it has equal quantities of fat and flour. Butter is the obvious choice of fat but butter and margarine mixed also give good flavour results.

The aim in making puff pastry is to produce a pastry that will rise evenly to tremendous heights – and here is where the rolling and folding procedures are so important. Follow the guidelines and tips below for good results:

★ Have everything as cool as possible before you start and use iced water

★ Chill the pastry thoroughly between rollings and before final use

★ Turning the pastry refers to a quarter-turn, To remember the position of your pastry during chilling, try to visualise your pastry as a closed book with the front facing upwards – so the long folded side will always be on the left hand side before you start to roll it out

★ The best way to remember the number of turns completed is to press the number of times in light dents on the top of the pastry

★ Allow the pastry to rest for about 2 hours before rolling out to the required shape. It will keep for about 3 days in the refrigerator if wrapped in cling film or foil

★ Bake sheets of puff pastry on a dampened baking tray wherever possible – the steam produced helps the pastry to rise

Basic Puff Pastry

Makes 4 pie crusts, 2 double-crust pies or flans, 2 puff pastry parcels, 2 mille feuilles, 2 medium pastry plaits or jalousies, 8–12 pasties or envelopes, 2 large vol-au-vents or about 50 cocktail nibbles

450g (1 lb) strong plain flour
pinch of salt
450g (1 lb) butter or butter and
  margarine mixed

300ml (½ pint) iced water
1 tablespoon lemon juice

Sift the flour and salt into a mixing bowl. Cut off 50g (2 oz) of the block of butter and add to the flour. Shape the remaining butter into an oblong about 2cm (¾ inch) thick and chill thoroughly.

Rub the 50g (2 oz) butter into the flour with the fingertips until the mixture resembles fine breadcrumbs. Stir in the water and lemon juice and bind to a firm but manageable dough. Turn onto a lightly-floured surface and knead lightly until smooth and elastic. Shape into a ball and slash the ball into four segments almost completely through the bottom. Open out the flaps of pastry and roll out until about 2cm (¾ inch) thick. Place the slab of butter in the centre of the pastry and fold over the flaps of pastry to completely enclose. Press the joins gently with a rolling pin to seal.

Roll out again to a rectangle 40 × 20cm (16 × 8 inches). Mark the pastry into three sections using the back of a knife. Fold the bottom third of pastry up and over the centre third of pastry and fold the top third of pastry down to cover both of these layers. Seal the edges together carefully with the side of the rolling pin and give the pastry a quarter-turn clockwise. Chill the pastry, wrapped in cling film or foil, for 30 minutes before rolling and folding again. Repeat the rolling and folding process a further 5 times. Finally chill for 2 hours before using.

After shaping, cook in a preheated hot oven (220°C, 425°F, Gas Mark 7), or according to specific recipe instructions.

FREEZING
Puff pastry can be frozen for up to 6 months. Thaw overnight in the refrigerator before using or for 1½–2 hours at room temperature.

Rough Puff Pastry

Rough puff pastry is similar in appearance to puff pastry but the similarities end there. While puff pastry involves adding the butter to the basic dough in a block, in rough puff pastry the butter is cut into small pieces and mixed with the flour and liquid to make a rough dough. The lumps of butter are then gradually eliminated by a series of rollings and folding. Rough puff pastry is certainly the simpler of the two pastries to make and quicker too. Follow the recipe guidelines and hints below for perfect results:

★ Have everything as cool as possible before you start
★ Chill the pastry thoroughly between rollings
★ When folding the pastry, brush away any loose flour sticking to the dough – too much flour will alter the proportions of ingredients
★ If the pastry starts to soften too much then chill immediately – you will probably only be able to roll the dough out twice at any one time
★ Turning the pastry refers to a quarter-turn. To remember the position of your pastry during chilling, try to visualise your pastry as a closed book with the front facing upwards – so the long folded side will always be on the left-hand side before you start to roll it out
★ The best way to remember the number of turns completed is to press the number of times in light dents on the top of the pastry
★ Allow the dough to rest for 1 hour before rolling out to the required shape
★ Bake sheets of rough puff pastry on a dampened baking tray wherever possible – the steam produced helps the pastry to rise

Basic Rough Puff Pastry

Makes 1 large pie crust, 4 medium-sized pasties, 36 small cocktail nibbles

175g (6 oz) butter   *150ml (¼ pint) iced water*
225g (8 oz) plain flour   *1 teaspoon lemon juice*
pinch of salt

Cut the butter into small walnut-sized pieces and place in a mixing bowl. Sift the flour and salt into the bowl. Stir in the water and lemon juice and, with a knife or the fingertips, gently mix together. Take care at this point not to break up the pieces of butter.

Turn onto a lightly-floured surface and knead very lightly and shape into a rectangular brick shape. Roll out on a lightly-floured surface to a long strip about 30 × 10cm (12 × 4 inches).

Mark the pastry into three sections using the back of a knife. Fold the bottom third of pastry up and over the centre third of pastry and fold the top third of pastry down to cover both of these layers. Seal the edges together carefully with the side of the rolling pin and give the pastry a quarter-turn clockwise.

Repeat this rolling and folding procedure four more times, chilling between each rolling and folding. Finally chill for 1 hour before using.

After shaping, cook in a preheated hot oven (220°C, 425°F, Gas Mark 7), or according to the specific recipe instructions.

FREEZING
Rough puff pastry can be frozen for up to 6 months. Thaw overnight in the refrigerator before using.

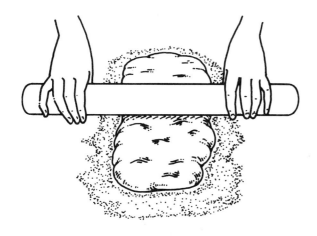

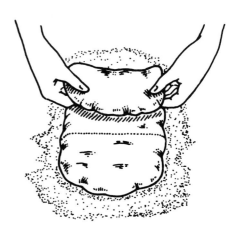

continued on page 30

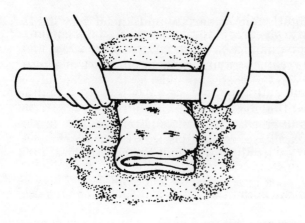

Danish Pastry

Danish pastry is a yeasted pastry most famously used for light, flaky Danish pastries. The recipe below is simple to make and the resulting pastry will be especially light if the procedures for folding and shaping are followed carefully.

Makes 16 pastries

15g (½ oz) fresh yeast or
  2 teaspoons dried yeast
6 tablespoons warm water
40g (1½ oz) castor sugar
275g (10 oz) plain flour

pinch of salt
25g (1 oz) lard
1 large (size 1, 2) egg
½ teaspoon vanilla essence
175g (6 oz) chilled butter

Cream the fresh yeast with the water and 15g (½ oz) of the sugar and leave in a warm place for 5–10 minutes until frothy. If using dried yeast, dissolve 15g (½ oz) of the sugar in the water and sprinkle over the yeast. Stir well then leave in a warm place for 10–15 minutes until frothy.

Sift the flour and salt into a mixing bowl. Rub the lard into the flour with the fingertips until the mixture resembles fine breadcrumbs. Beat the egg with the remaining sugar and vanilla essence. Add to the flour with the yeast mixture and mix to a fairly stiff dough. Turn onto a lightly-floured surface and knead until smooth and elastic. Wrap in cling film and chill for 15 minutes.

Meanwhile, cut the butter into eight thin slices, about 5mm (¼ inch) thick.

Roll out the pastry on a lightly-floured surface to a rectangle about 20 × 38cm (8 × 15 inches). Place four of the butter slices in the centre of the rectangle as shown in Diagram 1. Fold the left-hand half of the dough over the butter and seal the edges with the edge of a rolling pin, see Diagram 2. Place the remaining butter slices on top and fold over the right-hand half of the dough, see Diagram 3, and seal the edges. Roll out the dough to a rectangle about 40 × 15cm (16 × 6 inches). Fold both of the shorter edges to the centre as in Diagram 4 then one half on top of the other to make a four-layered piece of dough, see Diagram 5. Wrap in cling film and chill for about 30 minutes.

After chilling, roll out the pastry on a lightly-floured surface to a rectangle about 40 × 15cm (16 × 6 inches) and repeat the folding procedures as in Diagrams 4 and 5. Chill for 30 minutes then repeat this sequence once more. Finally chill for 1½ hours. The pastry is then ready to shape (see page 77) and fill for traditional Danish pastries.

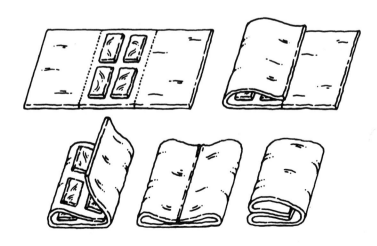

FILLINGS FOR DANISH PASTRIES

Sufficient for 16 assorted pastries (for 16 of the same treble the quantities below)

Almond paste: Mix 25g (1 oz) ground almonds with ½ small (size 6) beaten egg, 1 tablespoon castor sugar and 1 drop almond essence.

Vanilla cream: Mix ½ small (size 6) beaten egg with 1 teaspoon castor sugar and 1 teaspoon flour. Gradually add 50ml (2 fl oz) milk and cook over a low heat until smooth and thick. Allow to cool then beat in 2 drops vanilla essence.

Cinnamon sugar: Beat together 15g (½ oz) butter and 15g (½ oz) castor sugar. Add ½ teaspoon ground cinnamon, mixing well.

Apple and raisin: Mix ½ small peeled and grated apple with 1 tablespoon brown sugar, a small knob of butter, 15g (½ oz) raisins and a little grated orange rind.

PROVING DANISH PASTRIES

Place the shaped Danish pastries on lightly-greased baking trays and cover with oiled polythene or cling film. Leave in a warm place to rise until puffy, about 20–30 minutes. Remove the polythene and brush with beaten egg to glaze.

COOKING DANISH PASTRIES

After proving the pastries, cook in a preheated hot oven (220°C, 425°F, Gas Mark 7) for 10–15 minutes until cooked to a light golden brown. Allow to cool on a wire rack.

Flaky Pastry

Another pastry similar to puff, flaky pastry is generally used where a light flaky pastry is required without the need to rise to great heights. It is used in many sweet pastries like Eccles cakes and fruit-filled dumplings but can be used to top savoury meat and vegetable pies.

Follow the hints and tips under Puff Pastry and Rough Puff Pastry (see page 25) for good results.

Makes 12 Eccles cakes, 36 cocktail nibbles, 1 large pie crust or 4 medium pasties

225g (8 oz) plain flour	*8 tablespoons iced water*
pinch of salt	*1 teaspoon lemon juice*
175g (6 oz) butter	

Sift the flour and salt into a mixing bowl. Cream the butter on a plate until soft then divide into four equal portions. Add one portion to the flour and rub in with the fingertips until the mixture resembles fine breadcrumbs. Add the water and lemon juice and mix to a soft, elastic dough.

Turn onto a lightly-floured surface and knead until smooth and free from cracks. Roll out on a lightly-floured surface to a rectangle three times as long as it is wide. Lightly mark the pastry into three sections using the back of a knife.

Using a second portion of butter dot the butter in small flakes over the top two-thirds of the pastry rectangle. Fold the bottom

third of pastry up and over the centre third of pastry and fold the top third of pastry down to cover the centre third. Seal the edges lightly with the side of the rolling pin. Give the pastry a quarter turn and re-roll as before to a rectangle three times as long as it is wide. Repeat with the third portion of butter then chill for 20 minutes.

Finally repeat with the final portion of butter and chill for 30 minutes before using.

Cook in a preheated moderately hot oven (200°C, 400°F, Gas Mark 6) until well risen and golden brown, or according to the specific recipe instructions.

FREEZING
Freeze flaky pastry for up to 6 months. Thaw for at least 1½ hours at room temperature before using.

Choux Pastry

Choux pastry is perhaps one of the most intriguing pastries to make because it hardly looks like a pastry at all until it is cooked. Uncooked it looks like a thick, close-textured paste made of flour, eggs and water but when cooked becomes a crisp, hollow, delicate case risen to great heights and ready to fill with tempting mixtures.

The basic choux paste is not difficult to make or cook if you follow the basic recipe, but several guidelines should be followed to achieve excellent results:

★ Always weigh the ingredients accurately
★ Sift the flour with the salt first
★ Always allow the fat to melt before you bring the water to the boil (if you don't the water will evaporate and the proportions of ingredients will change)
★ Always beat the mixture until it is thick and smooth and leaves the sides of the pan clean
★ Allow the paste to cool slightly before adding the eggs. If they are added while the paste is too hot they may cook and set and therefore be unable to add air into the paste
★ Beat the eggs in gradually to trap as much air as possible into the mixture
★ Ensure that the oven is at the desired temperature before adding the pastry. A high heat is needed to produce steam immediately to cause the pastry to rise
★ Make sure the choux is thoroughly cooked before removing from the oven. Test by pinching slightly – the pastry should not feel the slightest bit soft. To make sure, pierce a little hole in the side to allow the steam to escape and return to the oven for a few minutes more
★ Bake choux pastry on a dampened baking tray wherever possible – the steam produced helps the pastry to rise
★ To produce light results when frying choux pastry, heat the oil in a deep-fat fryer or saucepan to 180°C (350°F) and fry until firm and golden. Drain on absorbent kitchen towel

Choux pastry has an almost limitless number of uses for both sweet and savoury dishes. We are all familiar with the well-known éclairs, cream puffs and profiteroles but other sweet uses include deep-fried choux pieces, beignets, sweet filled rings of choux, gougères and that choux pastry concoction – Gâteau St Honoré. Savoury uses are just as varied from savoury gougères, cheese choux balls for cocktail nibbles to savoury crisp 'dumplings' for topping casseroles and hot pots.

Ideally eat choux pastry dishes on the day they are made. You can, however, keep baked unfilled choux pastry for a day or two if stored, when quite cold, in an airtight tin. The pastry will soften when the filling is added so always fill at the very last possible moment.

Basic Choux Pastry

Makes 8–10 puffs, 12 éclairs, 1 puff ring or gougère, 12 choux swans or 30 profiteroles

65g (2½ oz) plain flour
pinch of salt
50g (2 oz) butter or margarine

150ml (¼ pint) water
2 eggs, beaten

Sift the flour and salt into a mixing bowl. Cut the butter or margarine into small pieces and place in a saucepan with the water. Heat slowly to melt the butter then bring up to a fast boil. Immediately add all of the flour and beat for 1 minute over the heat. Remove from the heat and beat until very smooth and the mixture forms a ball and leaves the sides of the pan clean. Allow to cool slightly.

Add the egg, a little at a time, beating well after each addition until the paste is smooth and glossy. An electric mixer can be used to do this. Always add the egg gradually otherwise the choux pastry will be too soft and not firm enough to shape. After shaping, cook in a preheated hot oven (220°C, 425°F, Gas Mark 7).

VARIATIONS
Sweet choux pastry: Prepare and cook as above but add 1 teaspoon castor sugar to the water and butter mixture.
Ham choux pastry: Prepare and cook as above but beat 50g (2 oz) finely chopped cooked ham into the choux paste while still warm.
Cheesy choux pastry: Prepare and cook as above but beat 50g (2 oz) grated strong-flavoured cheese into the choux paste while still warm.
Herby choux pastry: Prepare and cook as above but beat 2 teaspoons chopped fresh herbs of your choice or 1 teaspoon dried herbs into the choux paste while still warm.
Orange or lemon choux pastry: Prepare and cook as above but beat the grated rind of 1 small lemon or orange into the choux paste while still warm.
Bacon choux pastry: Prepare and cook as above but beat 50g (2 oz) finely-chopped cooked bacon into the choux paste while still warm.
Onion choux pastry: Prepare and cook as above but beat 1 small chopped cooked onion into the choux paste while still warm.
Fruity choux pastry: Prepare and cook as above but beat 50g (2 oz) chopped dried or glacé fruits into the choux paste while still warm.

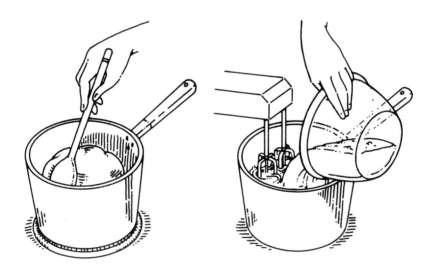

FREEZING

Choux pastry can be shaped and frozen before baking – thaw completely before baking when required. Alternatively bake then freeze and refresh in the oven for a few minutes after thawing and before filling.

Suet Crust Pastry

This is the rich, spongy and addictive pastry used to make roly-poly puddings, sweet and savoury pies and dumplings. It can be boiled, baked and steamed – although care must be taken with baking otherwise a hard and brittle crust may form. Long baking times should be avoided so use pre-cooked fillings when baking suet crust pastry.

Suet crust pastry is a simple pastry to make and is unusual since it uses self-raising flour as opposed to the normal plain flour for pastries. It needs the raising agent in self-raising flour to achieve its light spongy texture. The recipe below uses shredded packet suet but you can use fresh. If using fresh then choose beef or kidney suet and finely chop or grate before use. Toss in a little flour to prevent it sticking together. For a lighter suet crust pastry add breadcrumbs (see recipe below).

Basic Suet Crust Pastry

Makes enough to line a 900-ml (1½-pint) pudding basin, a medium-sized roly-poly or about 16 dumplings

225g (8 oz) self-raising flour
½ teaspoon salt
freshly ground black pepper to
  taste

100g (4 oz) shredded suet
about 150ml (¼ pint) cold
  water

Sift the flour, salt and pepper into a mixing bowl. Stir in the suet. Add the water and mix quickly using a round-bladed knife, or the fingertips of one hand, to form a light, elastic dough. Transfer to a lightly-floured surface and knead lightly until smooth and free from cracks. Roll out to 5mm (¼ inch) thickness and use as required.

Steam sweet and savoury puddings for about 2½–3 hours and bake roly-poly puddings in a preheated moderately hot oven (200°C, 400°F, Gas Mark 6) for 45 minutes, or according to specific recipe instructions. Dumplings, when placed in simmering casseroles, stews or soups, take about 25 minutes to cook.

VARIATIONS
Light suet crust pastry: Prepare and cook as above but add 50g (2 oz) fresh white breadcrumbs with the suet. Bind together with a little extra water to produce a suet crust pastry with a lighter texture.
Onion suet crust pastry: Prepare and cook as above but add ½ small chopped or grated onion with the suet.

Herby suet crust pastry: Prepare and cook as above but add 1-2 teaspoons chopped fresh herbs of your choice or ½-1 teaspoon dried herbs of your choice with the suet.

FREEZING
Not recommended

Hot Water Crust Pastry

Hot water crust pastry is essentially an English pastry used to make raised pies and picnic or buffet table fare. As a pastry it is quite unique in that the fat and water are heated together before being combined with the dry ingredients and it must be used while still warm and pliable. The result is a deliciously rich pastry that produces a handsome brown crust. The pastry must be allowed to cool completely after cooking and then a jellied stock is usually poured through a hole in the crust into the savoury filling.

Hot water crust pastry can be used to make small pork pies to large buffet table centre pieces and it is one of the easiest pastries to mould into both intricate or bold shapes. Raise the pastry by hand or use special shaped, hinged and loose-bottomed tins for easy release and perfect shaping. For foolproof results follow the tips below:

★ Heat the fat and water together to just boiling point then remove quickly from the heat. Heating too long will cause evaporation of the water and there will be insufficient liquid to bind the dry ingredients. This will produce a pastry that has a hard tough texture
★ Mix the hot mixture with the dry ingredients thoroughly – this helps to develop the gluten in the flour. Knead well to develop the gluten further. A short resting time at the end of kneading will also help
★ Keep any pieces of dough not being rolled out immed-iately covered and in a warm place. If the dough cools too much, it cannot be easily moulded and tends to crack

Makes 1 (450-g/1-lb) loaf-shaped pie, 1 (15-cm/6-inch) round pie or 4 individual double-crust pies

350g (12 oz) plain flour　　*150ml (¼ pint) milk or milk*
1 teaspoon salt　　　　　　　*and water mixed*
100g (4 oz) lard　　　　　　　*beaten egg to glaze*

Sift the flour and salt into a mixing bowl. Heat the lard and liquid in a pan gently until the fat melts. Bring quickly to the boil then pour at once into the dry ingredients. Mix quickly to make a fairly soft dough.

Turn onto a lightly-floured surface and knead until smooth, elastic and free from cracks. The dough should not appear streaky at this point. Use the dough quickly. Keep any reserved pastry in a warm bowl, covered, so that it does not harden on standing. Brush with beaten egg to glaze after shaping.

Cook in a preheated moderately hot oven (200°C, 400°F, Gas Mark 6) for 30 minutes then reduce the oven temperature to moderate (180°C, 350°F, Gas Mark 4) for the remainder of the cooking time, or cook according to specific recipe instructions.

Wholemeal Hot Water Crust Pastry

Makes 1 (450-g/1-lb) loaf-shaped pie, 1 (15-cm/6-inch) round pie or 4 individual double-crust pies

350g (12 oz) wholemeal plain flour
1 teaspoon salt
100g (4 oz) lard

200ml (7 fl oz) water or milk and water mixed
beaten egg to glaze

Sift the flour and salt into a mixing bowl. Heat the lard and liquid in a pan gently until the fat melts. Bring quickly to the boil then pour at once into the dry ingredients. Mix quickly to make a fairly soft dough.

Turn onto a lightly-floured surface and knead until smooth and elastic. The dough should not appear streaky at this point. Use the dough quickly. Keep any reserved pastry in a warm bowl, covered, so that it does not harden on standing. Brush with beaten egg to glaze after shaping.

Cook in a preheated moderately hot oven (200°C, 400°F, Gas Mark 6) for 30 minutes then reduce the oven temperature to moderate (180°C, 350°F, Gas Mark 4) for the remainder of the cooking time, or cook according to the specific recipe instructions.

Raised Pie Pastry

Very similar to hot water crust, this pastry is enriched with egg so that a delicious golden crisp crust is produced on baking.

Makes 1 (13-cm/5-inch) round pie

275g (10 oz) plain flour
½ teaspoon salt
1 egg yolk

150ml (¼ pint) milk or milk and water mixed
75g (3 oz) lard

Sift the flour and salt into a mixing bowl. Add the egg yolk and toss lightly in the flour. Heat the liquid and lard gently until the fat melts. Bring quickly to the boil then pour at once into the dry ingredients. Mix quickly to make a fairly soft dough.

Turn onto a lightly-floured surface and knead until smooth and elastic. Knead well to incorporate the egg yolk evenly. Use the dough quickly. Keep any reserved pastry in a warm bowl, covered, so that it does not harden on standing. Brush with beaten egg to glaze after shaping if liked.

Cook in a preheated moderately hot oven (200°C, 400°F, Gas Mark 6) for 30 minutes then reduce the oven temperature to moderate (180°C, 350°F, Gas Mark 4) for the remainder of the cooking time, or cook according to specific recipe instructions.

Phyllo or Strudel Pastry

This is a wafer-thin pastry that is popular throughout Europe. It is used in the classic sweet Greek baklava and in German or Austrian strudel pastries. It is a time and energy-consuming pastry to make but can be bought ready-prepared in delicatessen shops when time is at a premium.

Not an everyday pastry, the following tips should be observed for good results:

★ Always use warm ingredients and equipment – this encourages the development of the gluten
★ Unlike other pastries, beat and knead the dough vigorously – this also develops the gluten so that it can be stretched to a paper-thin dough
★ You will learn to recognise when the dough has been kneaded sufficiently – it will become less sticky, increasingly resilient and very smooth and silky
★ Use the fists of the hands to stretch the dough if you have long finger nails that are likely to puncture the dough

Makes 6 (25-cm/10-inch) sheets

225g (8 oz) strong plain flour
½ teaspoon salt
1 egg, beaten
2 tablespoons oil
¼ teaspoon lemon juice
5 tablespoons tepid water
25g (1 oz) butter, melted

Sift the flour and salt into a mixing bowl. Mix the egg with the oil and lemon juice. Add to the flour mixture and mix, with a fork, to a soft dough, adding the water as you mix. Using the hands, work the dough into a ball in the bowl then turn onto a lightly-floured surface. Knead vigorously for 15 minutes. When

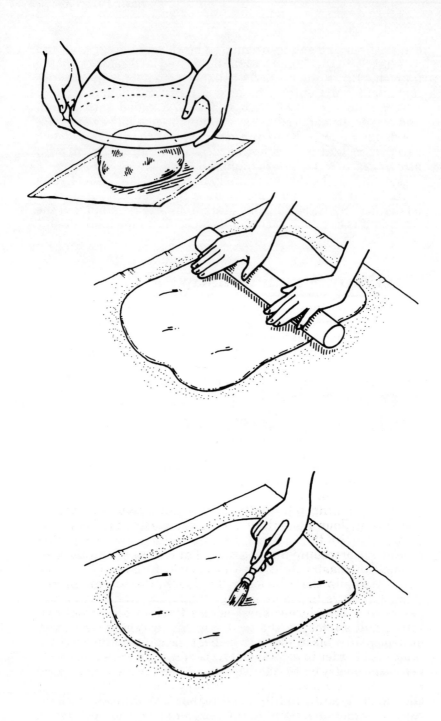

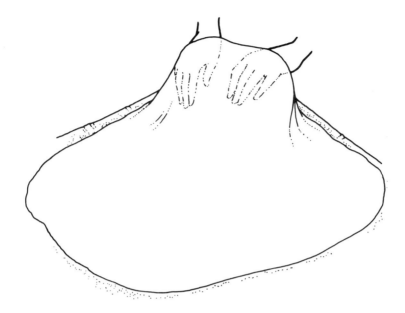

ready the dough will feel smooth, elastic and quite silky to the touch. Shape into a ball and cover with a warmed bowl. Leave to rest for 30 minutes.

Warm a rolling pin and prepare a large cloth by dusting lightly with flour. Place the pastry on the cloth and roll out until 3mm (⅛ inch) thick. Turn and lift the pastry during this rolling out procedure making sure that it does not stick.

Brush the pastry lightly with the melted butter. Flour your hands and slip them beneath the dough. Stretch the pastry from the centre to the outer edge by pulling and teasing the pastry to a translucent sheet across the knuckles. Continue lifting and stretching the pastry in this way until the sheet measures 75 × 50cm (30 × 20 inches). Trim away the slightly thickened border to give a neat rectangle of an even thickness. Leave the pastry on the cloth for about 15 minutes to rest before using. Cook in a preheated moderately hot oven (190°C, 375°F, Gas Mark 5) until lightly browned, or according to specific recipe instructions. Store in the refrigerator for up to 1 day.

FREEZING
Freeze phyllo or strudel pastry for up to 6 months.

Yeast Pastry

Makes 1 (25-cm/10-inch) flan or large pizza base

1 teaspoon sugar
150ml (¼ pint) warm milk
7g (¼ oz) fresh yeast

225g (8 oz) plain flour
1 teaspoon salt
50g (2 oz) butter

Mix the sugar with the milk and yeast and leave in a warm place until well-risen and frothy.

Sift the flour and salt into a mixing bowl. Cut the butter into small pieces and rub into the flour with the fingertips until the mixture resembles fine breadcrumbs. Add the yeast liquid and mix to a fairly soft but manageable dough.

Turn onto a lightly-floured surface and knead until smooth and elastic, about 5 minutes. Place in a bowl and cover with polythene or cling film and leave until doubled in size. Knead again for 2–3 minutes before rolling out to use.

Cook in a preheated hot oven (220°C, 425°F, Gas Mark 7) until well-risen and golden brown, or according to specific recipe instructions.

Scone Pastry

Scone pastry is one of the simplest quick-mix type pastries to make. Use it as a delicious base for flans and pizzas.

Makes 1 medium-sized family pizza base, 1 (23-cm/9-inch) flan or 1 large pie crust

225g (8 oz) self-raising flour
½ teaspoon salt

50g (2 oz) butter
7 tablespoons milk

Sift the flour and salt into a mixing bowl. Cut the butter into small pieces and rub into the flour with the fingertips until the mixture resembles fine breadcrumbs. Add the milk, all at once, and mix with a round-bladed knife to a soft dough.

Turn out onto a lightly-floured surface and knead lightly until smooth and free from cracks. Roll out on a lightly-floured surface and cook in a preheated moderately hot oven (190°C, 375°F, Gas Mark 5) or according to specific recipe instructions.

VARIATION
Sweet scone pastry: Prepare and cook as above but add 25g (1 oz) castor sugar to the rubbed-in mixture prior to binding with milk.

44

Potato Pastry

Little known or used in Britain, potato pastry is a favourite in Austria, Bavaria and in many parts of Germany. It is mainly used to make knödels or dumplings both baked and boiled as well as sweet and savoury roulades. To make a sweet potato pastry simply add sugar to taste to the recipe below.

Makes 4-6 large dumplings

400g (14 oz) floury potatoes
100g (4 oz) plain flour
25g (1 oz) semolina

1 egg, beaten
25g (1 oz) butter
¼ teaspoon salt

Cook the potatoes in their skins in boiling salted water until soft. Drain, allow to cool slightly then peel and mash to a smooth purée. Leave to cool.

Add the flour and semolina to the cooled potato and mix well. Add the egg, butter and salt, beating well until very smooth. An electric food beater can be used to do this. Roll out on a lightly-floured surface and use as required.

Brioche Dough

Brioche dough is used, of course, to make delicious brioche buns but can also be used to make French-type loaves that can be sliced and toasted to make crisp, sweet rusks. It is also served in France as a sweet bread type pudding with a custard or sweet white sauce.

Makes about 20 small brioches

500g (1 lb 2 oz) strong plain flour
pinch of salt
25g (1 oz) castor sugar
25g (1 oz) fresh yeast

150ml (¼ pint) hand-hot milk
4 eggs, beaten
225g (8 oz) butter, softened
beaten egg to glaze

Sift the flour and salt into a mixing bowl. Make a well in the centre of the flour mixture. Cream the sugar and yeast together and mix with the milk. Add to the well in the flour with the eggs and beat well to combine and form a fairly soft dough.

Turn onto a lightly-floured surface and knead until very smooth and elastic, about 5–10 minutes. Add the butter and knead again until smooth. Chill until the dough is firm enough to handle.

Divide the dough into 25-g (1-oz) pieces. Divide each piece into two-third and one-third pieces. Roll each of the larger pieces into a ball and place in the bases of greased individual brioche moulds. Brush with a little beaten egg. Roll the remaining smaller pieces into small balls and place on top of the larger balls to make cottage loaf shapes. Brush again with beaten egg to glaze. Cover with polythene or cling film and leave in a warm place to rise until they reach the tops of the moulds, about 30 minutes.

Cook in a preheated moderately hot oven (200°C, 400°F, Gas Mark 6) for about 12-15 minutes. Allow to cool on a wire rack.

Pizza Dough

Makes 2 (23-cm/9-inch) pizzas

1 teaspoon sugar
15g (½ oz) fresh yeast or
  2 teaspoons dried
150ml (¼ pint) warm water

225g (8 oz) plain flour
1½ teaspoons salt
oil

Mix the sugar with the yeast and water. Leave in a warm place until well risen and frothy, about 15 minutes.

Meanwhile sift the flour and salt into a mixing bowl. Add the yeast liquid and mix to a smooth dough. Turn onto a lightly-floured surface and knead until smooth and elastic, about 5–10 minutes. Form into a ball and rub the surface very lightly with a couple of drops of oil. Cover with polythene or cling film and leave in a warm place until doubled in size.

Turn onto a lightly-floured surface and knead again for 2–3 minutes. Divide the dough into two equal pieces and roll each out to fit a 23-cm (9-inch) pizza pan or greased baking tray. Cover again with polythene or cling film and leave in a warm place for about 20 minutes. Top with the chosen ingredients and cook in a preheated hot oven (230°C, 450°F, Gas Mark 8) until cooked and golden, or according to specific recipe instructions.

Chapati Dough

Chapatis are thin flat unleavened pastry-type breads, originating in India. They are usually served with curries and other spicy dishes.

Makes about 14

675g (1½ lb) wholemeal flour
water to bind

4 tablespoons white plain flour

Mix the wholemeal flour with sufficient water in a mixing bowl to make a firm but pliable dough – this will depend very much upon the age of the flour and conditions under which it has been stored. Turn onto a lightly-floured surface and knead until smooth and free from cracks. Cover and leave to rest for 30 minutes.

Divide the dough into about fourteen pieces and roll each into a small ball. Dip the balls in the white flour then roll out to make fourteen thin, oval-shaped chapatis, about 5mm (¼ inch) thick.

Heat a heavy-based griddle or pan until very hot. Add a chapati and cook for 20 seconds, turn over and cook for a further 20 seconds. The chapati should puff up and colour slightly during this time. Cook the remaining chapatis in the same way. Serve warm with butter.

Pitta Dough

Pitta bread is a tasty flat pastry bread that comes from the Middle East. After cooking it is placed in a teacloth or wrapped in foil so that it softens and collapses, leaving the characteristic shallow pocket for which it is widely known. Fill pitta bread with mixed salad ingredients or kebabs for delicious meals.

Makes 8 pittas

450g (1 lb) strong white flour	*15g (½ oz) fresh yeast*
½ teaspoon salt	*about 300ml (½ pint) tepid water*

Sift the flour and salt into a large mixing bowl. Make a well in the centre. Blend the yeast with a little of the water until smooth then add the remaining water. Add the yeast liquid to the flour mixture and mix to a stiff but manageable dough. Turn onto a lightly-floured surface and knead until smooth and elastic. Place in the bowl, cover with polythene or cling film and leave in a warm place until the dough has doubled in size. Turn onto a lightly-floured surface and knead again for 2–3 minutes.

Divide the dough into eight equal-sized pieces and knead each lightly into a smooth ball. Roll each ball out to a 5mm (¼ inch) thick oval and place on baking trays. Cover with oiled polythene or cling film and leave in a warm place until spongy.

Meanwhile, heat two greased baking trays in a preheated hot oven (230°C, 450°F, Gas Mark 8). Place two pitta breads onto each baking tray and brush with a little cold water. Cook in the oven for 10 minutes. Remove from the baking trays and cool on a wire rack while cooking the remaining four pitta breads. When all are cooked, wrap in foil or in a teacloth and leave until quite cold. The pitta breads will soften and collapse during this time.

When cold, split the breads down one side to make the traditional pocket.

Tortilla Dough

A tortilla is a kind of Mexican pastry bread. A thin, flat cornbread, it is often served with spicy bean and meat mixtures like chilli. If fried on one side and used to encase a chilli and bean filling it becomes a *taco* and, more exotically, if stuffed, rolled and fried then coated with a sauce it becomes an *enchilada*.

Makes 12 tortillas

250g (9 oz) fine cornmeal   250ml (8 fl oz) tepid water
½ teaspoon salt

Mix the cornmeal and salt in a large mixing bowl. Gradually add the water and mix to a stiff but manageable dough. Knead in the bowl until smooth and free from cracks.

Divide the dough into twelve equal pieces and shape each into a small ball. Keep the balls covered with cling film to prevent drying out while you roll out each one. Flatten each ball with a rolling pin until 5mm (¼ inch) thick, then place between two sheets of waxed or greaseproof paper and roll out to 15-cm (6-inch) rounds.

Peel away the paper just prior to cooking. Place in a hot ungreased frying pan and cook for ½ minute or until the edges curl up. Turn the tortilla over with a spatula and press down gently with the spatula until bubbles form underneath it. Turn again and cook for a further 1 minute. Remove and stack on a sheet of foil while cooking the remaining tortillas.

Pâte L'eau

Pâte l'eau isn't so much a pastry as a sealing paste for sealing pâtés, slow-cooking casseroles and hot pots during cooking. It is simply a flour and water paste that is used to seal the base of a dish with its lid so that delicate juices and moisture cannot evaporate from the dish during cooking. After cooking, the seal is broken to serve.

Makes enough paste to seal 1 medium-sized pâté or casserole

5 tablespoons flour   iced water to blend

Mix the flour with enough water to make a thick paste. Using the fingers, spread the paste around the rim of the dish and its lid making an airtight seal. Follow specific cooking instructions then break the seal, which will have cooked crisp, to serve.

PASTRY TECHNIQUES

Preparing a Single-crust Pie Top

The filling of any single-crust pie will lose volume upon cooking. For this reason it is important to anchor the pie lid to the rim of the dish prior to cooking. Steam, rising from the sweet or savoury filling, will therefore raise the pastry crust to a high, firm dome without fear of collapse.

To prepare a single-crust pie top, roll out the prepared pastry on a lightly-floured surface to a round about 4cm (1½ inches) larger than the pie dish. Trim a 2.5-cm (1-inch) strip from the edge of the pastry to form a pastry collar.

Moisten the pie dish rim with water and press the pastry collar firmly onto the rim, overlapping the ends. Place any filling into the dish at this point.

Dampen the pastry rim with water so that the lid of the pie will stick to it. Carefully fold the pastry lid in half and position on top of the pie, unfolding to cover completely and neatly.

Press the lid and pastry collar firmly together and trim away any excess dough with a sharp knife. Position the blade of the knife upwards and outwards while doing this so that you leave a slightly overhanging edge to the crust that allows for shrinkage during cooking.

Seal the edges of the pastry by tapping the blade of the knife horizontally against the edge of the pie all round; known as 'knocking up'. This stops the pie crust and collar from separating during cooking.

Flute the edges of the pastry and decorate with any pastry trimmings as liked. See pages 91 to 93 for ideas. With a sharp knife, pierce the top in several places to allow any steam to escape. Glaze the pie and dust with sugar, poppy seeds, sesame seeds etc. as recommended. Cook according to recipe instructions.

Preparing a Double-crust Pie

The secret in making a perfect double-crust pie lies in keeping the base crisp not soggy. For this reason aim to choose fillings that are not too moist or thicken those that are prior to cooking. A thin coating of egg white on the pastry base will also prevent the juices from seeping into the dough.

To prepare a double-crust pie, first divide the prepared pastry in half, one for the pastry base and one for the top or crust. Roll out one of the pieces of pastry to a round large enough to line the base of the chosen dish or tin comfortably. Roll the pastry onto a floured rolling pin and then unroll it over the greased dish or tin. Carefully mould the pastry into the dish or tin with your fingers, taking care not to stretch the pastry. If the pastry breaks or becomes damaged in any area, then patch carefully with a bit of extra pastry.

Brush the pastry base with a little whisked egg white before adding the filling if liked. When this cooks in the oven, it forms a slight seal and glaze which prevents seepage into the pastry base. Top with the filling as liked and brush the pastry rim with water or beaten egg to dampen. Roll out the remaining piece of pastry to a round large enough to cover the pie and place over the filling.

Press the lid and pastry base together firmly and trim away any excess dough with a sharp knife. Position the blade of the knife upwards and outwards while doing this so that you leave a slightly overhanging edge to the crust that allows for shrinkage during cooking.

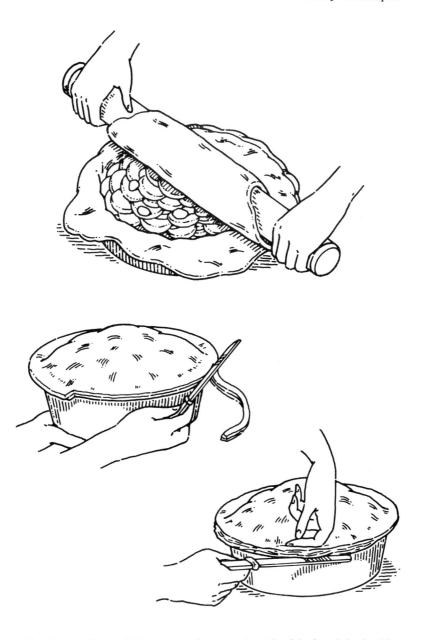

Seal the edges of the pastry by tapping the blade of the knife horizontally against the edge of the pie all round. This stops the pie crust and base from separating during cooking.

Flute the edges of the pastry and decorate with any pastry trimmings as liked. See pages 91 to 93 for ideas. With a sharp knife, pierce the top in several places to allow any steam to escape. Glaze the pie and dust with sugar, poppy seeds, sesame seeds etc. as recommended. Cook according to recipe instructions.

Lining a Flan Tin or Quiche Dish

Roll out the pastry on a lightly-floured surface to a round large enough to line the inside of the chosen flan tin or quiche dish. Lift by rolling the pastry loosely around the rolling pin then lay it over the flan tin and let it unroll.

Ease the pastry carefully into the corners of the flan tin, taking care not to stretch unnecessarily. Roll the rolling pin over the pastry to cut off excess pastry round the edges.

Press the pastry into the flan tin and pinch it slightly at the top, raising it above the edge to allow for shrinkage. Leave to rest for 20–30 minutes before cooking.

TO BAKE 'BLIND'

It is a good idea to bake a flan or quiche 'blind' before adding the filling since it prevents the bottom crust from becoming soggy or remaining undercooked. This partial pre-cooking is called baking 'blind'.

To bake 'blind', cut a square of foil or greaseproof paper slightly larger than the flan tin and use it to line the base and sides of the pastry-lined dish.

Weigh down with beans, pasta or rice if greaseproof paper is used. This weighs the pastry down so that it does not buckle up as it cooks.

Cook in a preheated moderately hot oven (200°C, 400°F, Gas Mark 6) for 10–15 minutes. Remove the foil or paper and beans and cook for a further 5 minutes. Add the filling if this needs cooking, then follow the specific recipe instructions.

If a completely baked pastry case is required for a recipe then bake for a further 15 minutes after removing the foil or paper and beans.

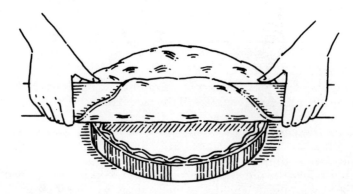

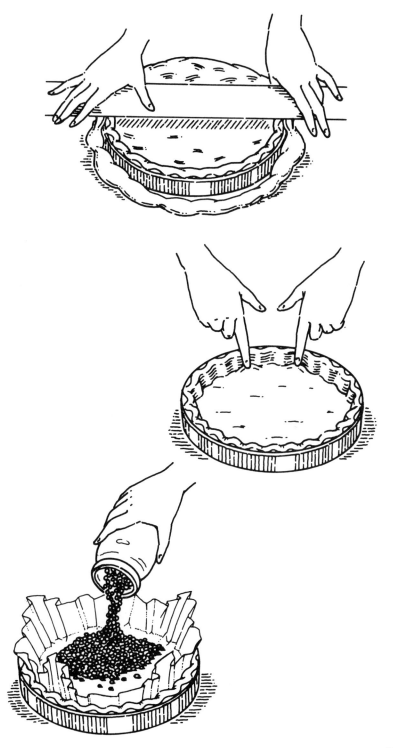

Preparing an Upside-down Fruit and Pastry Tart

It is easy to prepare a fruit tart by placing a layer of prepared pastry over a fruit filling, cooking it, then inverting the whole mixture onto a plate to serve. It becomes especially simple to prepare if you cook the fruit, where necessary, in the pan you intend to cook the whole tart. It is one of the simplest ways to prepare a fruit tart without the need to mould pastry into a tin.

Some fruits like apples do not require cooking before topping with the pastry crust, others like pears, peaches and plums need gentle poaching. Place the prepared fruit in the base of the prepared tin. Roll out the prepared pastry, shortcrust, puff, flaky and rough puff can be used, to a round about 5cm (2 inches) larger than the chosen tin. Prick thoroughly with a fork to allow any steam to escape during cooking and make a pastry border by folding over the edge of the dough by about 2.5cm (1 inch). Press the border flat with the back of a fork.

Lift the pastry over a rolling pin then place over the fruit mixture, with the folded edge down. Tuck the pastry rim in around the edges.

Cook in a preheated moderately hot oven (190°C, 375°F, Gas Mark 5) for 30–45 minutes, depending upon size, until golden brown, crisp and cooked through. Allow to cool slightly in the tin before inverting onto a plate to serve.

To prevent any juices from soaking into the crust making it soggy and difficult to serve, do not unmould until just before serving.

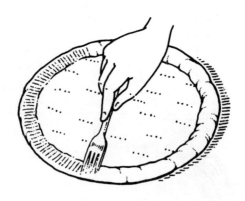

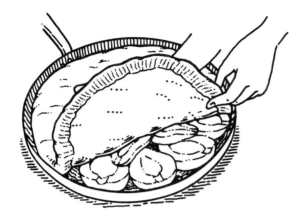

Preparing a Free-standing Pastry Case

Quite often you may like to bake a pastry case of an unusual size be it small or large or even an unusual shape. It is possible to make one without the need for a baking tin if you follow the technique below. The only limitation will be the size of your baking tray or oven.

Roll out the prepared pastry on a lightly-floured surface to a size and shape 5cm (2 inches) larger than the required one. Transfer to a greased or dampened baking tray and turn up the edges by carefully rolling over and pinching together the pastry so that it stands up to a height of about 2.5cm (1 inch).

Fill the pastry case with the chosen filling and cook according to the specific recipe instructions. As a guideline, a 25-cm (10-inch) free-standing pastry case filled with fruit slices and dusted with sugar will take approximately 50 minutes to cook in a preheated moderate oven (180°C, 350°F, Gas Mark 4). Allow to cool on a wire rack.

Lining Tartlet Moulds

Roll out the prepared pastry on a lightly-floured surface and with a pastry cutter, or the rim of a tin, cut out rounds of pastry large enough to fit the chosen tartlet moulds. Gently press the pastry rounds into the tartlet moulds with the thumbs. Start pressing into the moulds from the centre and working out to the sides. This eliminates any air trapped under the pastry which could cause the pastry cases to buckle on cooking.

Place the tartlet moulds onto a baking tray if necessary and prick the base and sides of the pastry thoroughly with a fork.

Fill with the chosen mixture and cook according to the specific recipe instructions. If baked tartlet cases are required, line the pastry-lined moulds with greaseproof paper and baking beans. Cook in a preheated moderately hot oven (190°C, 375°F, Gas Mark 5) for about 15 minutes until golden brown and cooked through. Remove beans, paper and tins. Allow to cool on a wire rack.

Preparing Pastry Boats or Lining Barquette Tins

Place fluted or plain boat-shaped moulds close together on a baking tray. Roll out the prepared pastry on a lightly-floured surface large enough to cover the moulds completely. Carefully lift the pastry over the moulds with a rolling pin.

Loosely cover the moulds taking great care not to stretch the pastry and encouraging the pastry to sink into the moulds. Take a small piece of pastry from one of the edges and roll into a small ball. Use this ball of pastry to pat and press the pastry into the moulds excluding any air.

Take a rolling pin and run it across the pastry-lined moulds, first in one direction and then in the other. The sharp edges of the moulds will cut through the pastry leaving a clean, neat edge. Re-use any pastry trimmings to make more pastry boats if liked.

Prick the sides and the bases of the moulds with a fork and use according to specific recipe instructions. For fully-baked pastry boats, line the pastry-lined moulds with greaseproof paper and baking beans. Cook in a preheated moderately hot oven (190°C, 375°F, Gas Mark 5) for 7–10 minutes. Remove beans, paper and tins. Allow to cool on a wire rack.

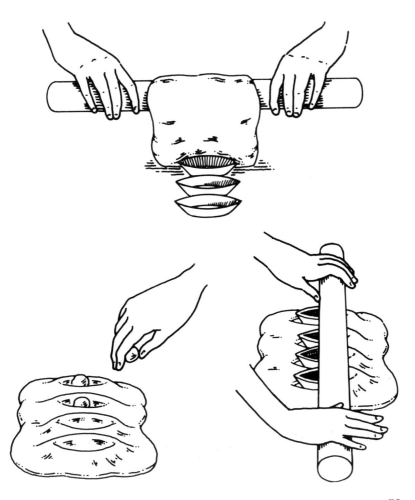

Preparing a Cheesecake Pastry Case

Two separate cooking operations are required in making a pastry-enclosed cheesecake because the cook is faced with a culinary dilemma. If the pastry crust is not pre-cooked before adding the filling the pastry base will generally remain uncooked and soggy after cooking. If the pastry case is cooked before adding the filling, it is liable to overbrown on the sides upon further cooking to set the filling.

The solution is to pre-cook the pastry base in one operation and then to add the pastry sides and filling to cook in a second.

Divide the prepared pastry in half. Roll out one half on the top of the base of the greased spring-form tin to be used, trimming away any excess pastry.

Prick the pastry thoroughly with a fork to prevent the base from rising and buckling unevenly during cooking. Cook in a preheated moderately hot oven (200°C, 400°F, Gas Mark 6) for 15 minutes until just golden.

Roll out the remaining pastry into one long strip long enough to line the sides of the chosen tin. Grease the sides of the tin and place the pastry strip around it, moulding it gently onto the base to seal. Seal the ends well by moulding together. Trim the edges with a sharp knife to give a neat finish.

Add the filling to the prepared pastry case and cook according to the specific recipe instructions. Allow the cheesecake to cool in its tin on a wire rack for at least 2 hours before carefully unmoulding.

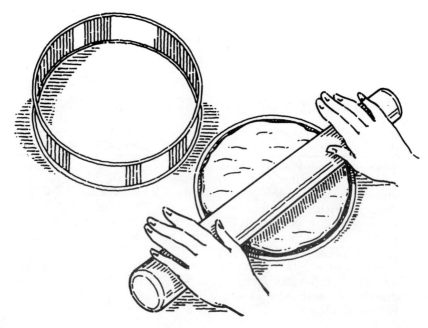

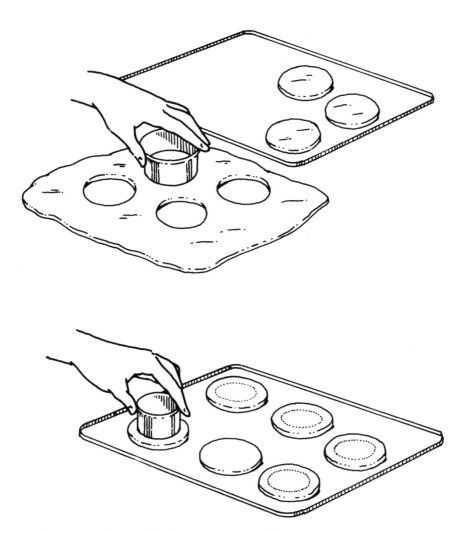

Preparing Vol-au-vent Cases

Roll out the prepared puff pastry to about 1cm (½ inch) thickness. Cut out rounds with a 7.5-cm (3-inch) cutter and place on a dampened baking tray.

Using a smaller 5-cm (2-inch) plain or fluted cutter, cut almost through to the base of the pastry to mark the lid. Brush the tops with beaten egg to glaze, taking care not to glaze the sides (this can prevent the pastry from rising) and cook in a preheated hot oven (230°C, 450°F, Gas Mark 8) for 10 minutes or until golden.

Remove the lids from the bases with a sharp knife and scoop out any soft pastry from the insides of the vol-au-vents and discard. Allow the bases and lids to cool on a wire rack. Fill just before serving.

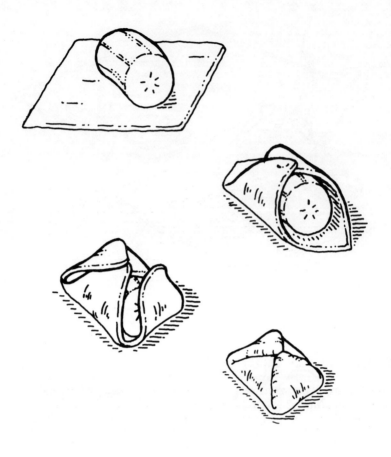

Preparing Pastry Dumplings

To make twelve small pastry dumplings using ¼ quantity puff pastry, roll out the prepared pastry on a lightly-floured surface to a rectangle 50 × 38cm (20 × 15 inches). Cut into twelve (13-cm/5-inch) squares.

Place a spoonful of the prepared filling in the centre of the squares. Bring the two opposite corners of the pastry together across the top of the filling. Overlap the ends of the dough over the top of the filling and press firmly to seal. Bring the remaining two corners to the centre and overlap them on top of the first two corners. Press firmly to seal.

Fold over the open edges slightly and press to seal. Brush with beaten egg to glaze and cook according to specific recipe instructions.

The same folding and sealing procedures can be used to make larger or smaller pastry dumplings with pastries other than puff.

Preparing a Roly-Poly

Using 1 quantity suet crust pastry, roll out the prepared pastry on a lightly-floured surface to a rectangle 25 × 30cm (10 × 12 inches). Spread or sprinkle with the chosen filling to within 2cm (¾ inch) of the edges. Brush the edges with water or a little milk. Turn in the edges on the two long sides and one short side and dampen again with water or milk. Roll up, from the short folded edge, like a Swiss roll. Wrap loosely in greased foil and place on a baking tray if baking. Twist the ends of the foil to seal. Bake or steam according to the specific recipe instructions.

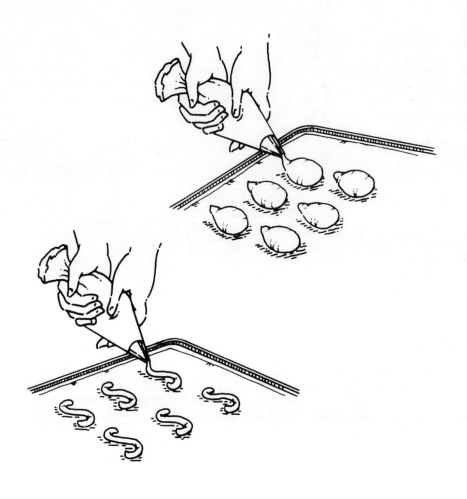

Preparing Choux Pastry Swans

Spoon two-thirds of the prepared choux pastry into a piping bag fitted with a 2-cm (¾-inch) plain nozzle and pipe large 'teardrops' of dough onto a greased and floured baking tray.

Place the remaining choux pastry in a piping bag fitted with a 5-mm (¼-inch) plain nozzle and pipe out small 'S' shapes onto another greased and floured baking tray.

Cook the swans in a preheated moderately hot oven (190°C, 375°F, Gas Mark 5) for 10–12 minutes until the 'S' shapes are well-risen and golden brown. Allow the 'S' shapes to cool on a wire rack and cook the 'teardrop' shapes for a further 20–25 minutes. Remove from the oven, pierce with a knife to allow any steam to escape then cook for a further 5 minutes to dry out. Cool on a wire rack.

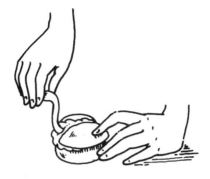

To assemble the swans, split each 'teardrop' bun in half horizontally with a sharp knife. Leave the base whole but cut the top into two halves. Fill the base with the chosen filling – confectioner's custard or whipped cream are traditional.

Place both pieces of the top back onto the base to represent wings. Position the 'S' shape neck into the filling between the point of the wings to complete. Dust with icing sugar before serving.

Preparing a Puff Pastry Patchwork

Roll out two-thirds of the prepared puff pastry to a large rectangle about 5mm (¼ inch) thick. Place on a dampened baking tray and prick thoroughly with a fork.

Roll out the remaining pastry and cut into long strips, 2.5cm (1 inch) wide. These are to be used to form a border for the pastry base and to partition the rectangle into sections. Brush the pastry edge with water and secure the strips to the border, trimming to ensure a neat fit. Brush the remaining strips with water and position on the base in a neat geometric pattern, trimming again to ensure a neat finish.

Brush the border and pastry strips with beaten egg to glaze and cook in a preheated hot oven (220°C, 425°F, Gas Mark 7) for 25–30 minutes until well-risen, golden brown and cooked through. Allow to cool on a wire rack.

Fill the individual sections with variations of jam, flavoured creams, fruits and candied mixtures. Serve as soon as possible while the pastry is still crisp.

Lining a Raised Pie Mould

Roll out three-quarters of the prepared hot water crust or raised pie pastry on a lightly-floured surface to about 5mm (¼ inch) thickness. Keep the remaining pastry covered and warm until required. Place the greased mould onto a baking tray and lift the rolled pastry into it. Press carefully into the mould, pressing the pastry into the corners and any indentations or pattern. Allow the pastry to stand about 5mm (¼ inch) above the rim of the mould. Add the filling and pack down well.

Roll out the remaining pastry on a lightly-floured surface. Dampen the pastry rim with water. Position the lid on the pie and pinch the edges together to seal. Trim, seal and flute decoratively. Cut a hole in the pie crust to allow any steam to escape during the cooking and brush with beaten egg to glaze.

Cook in a preheated moderately hot oven (200°C, 400°F, Gas Mark 6) for the first 30 minutes of the cooking time then reduce the oven temperature to moderate (180°C, 350°F, Gas Mark 4) and cook for the remaining time, or according to specific recipe instructions.

To test if the filling is cooked, insert a fine skewer through the hole in the crust and test for resistance.

The sides of the mould may be removed for the last 45 minutes of the cooking time then brushed with beaten egg to glaze so that they also can cook to a golden brown. Allow to cool slightly before filling with aspic or jellied stock if liked.

To fill the pie with aspic or jellied stock, pour through a funnel and the hole in the crust of the pie until full.

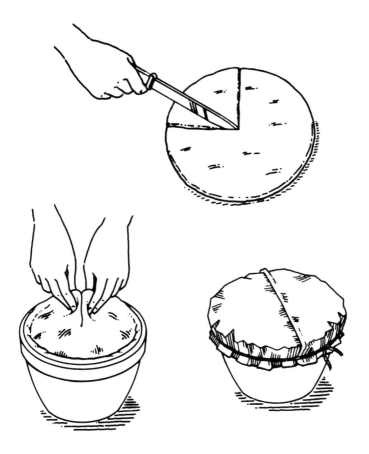

Lining a Pudding Basin with Suet Crust Pastry

Roll out the prepared suet crust pastry on a lightly-floured surface to a round about 5cm (2 inches) larger than the diameter of the chosen pudding basin (about 30cm/12 inches for a 1.2-litre/2-pint pudding basin). Cut a quarter section from the pastry round and reserve for a lid.

Lift the remaining piece of dough and carefully ease it into the basin, pinching the two cut edges together to seal and moulding the dough onto the base and around the sides of the basin.

Add the chosen filling. Roll out the remaining pastry to a round large enough to make a lid. Brush the pastry edges with water and cover with the pastry lid. Pinch the damp edges together firmly to seal. Trim away any excess pastry.

Cover either with a piece of pleated greaseproof paper and foil and tie with string, *or* a pleated piece of greaseproof paper and a pudding cloth. Tie the cloth securely under the rim with string then knot the opposite corners of the cloth together to form a handle for lifting the basin from the pan. (The pleated greaseproof paper and foil allow for expansion of the pastry and filling during cooking.)

A thick double-strength strip of foil may be placed under and up the sides of the pudding basin to ease lifting the basin from the pan if liked.

Preparing Pastry Horns

Roll out the prepared flaky, puff, rough puff or shortcrust pastry on a lightly-floured surface and cut into strips measuring 1 × 35cm (½ × 14 inches). Dampen one side of each pastry strip with water.

With the dry side of each pastry strip next to the metal, carefully wind each strip around the pastry horn mould, starting from the pointed end. Take care to overlap the pastry strip evenly and not to stretch the pastry unnecessarily. Trim away any excess pastry.

Place the prepared pastry horns on a greased or dampened baking tray with the loose end downwards to keep the horns neatly rolled. Chill for 30–60 minutes. Brush with beaten egg or milk to glaze and dust with icing sugar if sweet, and cook according to specific recipe instructions. Generally flaky, puff

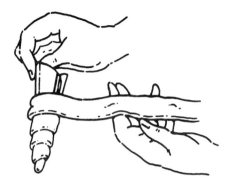

or rough puff pastry horns will be cooked in a preheated hot oven (220°C, 425°F, Gas Mark 7) for 25 minutes. Shortcrust pastry horns are usually cooked in a preheated moderately hot oven (200°C, 400°F, Gas Mark 6) for 20-25 minutes until golden and cooked through. Slip the horns from their tins about 3-4 minutes before the end of their cooking time and return to the oven to dry out. Allow to cool on a wire rack.

Fill the horns as required with either sweet or savoury fillings.

Preparing a Mille Feuille

Traditionally, and to live up to its name which translates as 'thousand leaves', a mille feuille is made of puff or rough puff pastry. You can however use shortcrust pastry to create the same pastry layered effect.

Roll out the prepared pastry on a lightly-floured surface into a large rectangle about 3mm (⅛ inch) thick. Using a sharp knife, cut the dough into three equal-sized rectangles and place on dampened baking trays. Use greased baking trays when using shortcrust pastry. Prick thoroughly with a fork, this ensures that the pastry rises evenly. A sharp knife is essential to get a good clean cut to aid rising. Chill for at least 30 minutes before cooking. Cook the pastry rectangles in a preheated hot oven (220°C, 425°F, Gas Mark 7) until crisp and golden, about 20 minutes, or follow specific recipe instructions. Allow to cool on a wire rack.

When cool, stack the pastry rectangles one upon another and, with a sharp knife, trim the edges so that all the rectangles are the same size. Crush any crumbs and reserve to decorate the top later if liked.

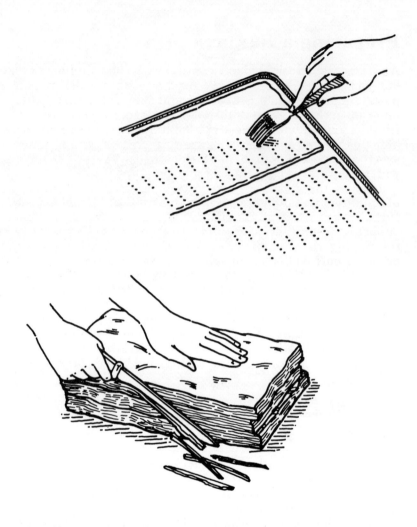

You can fill a mille feuille with any number of sweet or savoury fillings. Spread one rectangle with half of the chosen mixture and top with another layer of pastry. Spread in turn with the remaining filling and place the remaining rectangle on top. The basic mille feuille is then complete.

Decorate the mille feuille as liked. Sweet ones can be dusted with icing sugar and scored with a red-hot skewer, coated with glacé icing and dusted with the reserved pastry crumbs or decorated with fresh fruit. Savoury mille feuilles can be topped with fresh herbs or sliced vegetables or one of the rectangles can be baked with a sprinkling of sesame seeds, poppy seeds, grated cheese or herbs prior to cooking.

Preparing a Baklava

An authentic Greek baklava is made with thin phyllo pastry but you can get equally tasty results using strudel or puff pastry. A baklava is a honey, nut and spice filled pastry that relies upon the layering of thin pastry for its success. You can fill the baklava with almost any mixture of chopped nuts but almonds, walnuts or pistachios are the more typical. The honey syrup which literally drenches the pastry can also be flavoured with rose water, whole cloves or lemon slices if liked.

Roll out the prepared pastry on a lightly-floured surface to squares or rectangles large enough to fit the baking tin used. If you are using thin phyllo or strudel dough you will need about 20 sheets, if using puff pastry, about 4 sheets. Generously butter the baking tin then layer in half of the sheets of pastry, brushing each with melted butter.

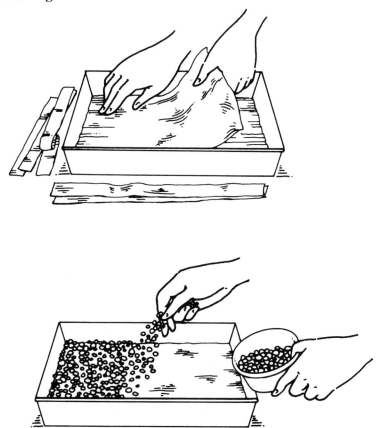

Top the pastry with the nut and honey filling as liked. Add the remaining sheets of pastry, each brushed as before with melted butter.

To mark the baklava into the traditional diamond or triangle pattern, score through the top layers of the pastry just down to the nut filling with a sharp knife. Cut the pastry into diamond shapes or triangles as liked giving a neat finish.

Cook in a preheated hot oven (200°C, 400°F, Gas Mark 6) according to specific recipe instructions, until crisp and golden.

Allow the baklava to cool a little in its tin before pouring over the hot prepared honey syrup. Cut the pastry into diamond or triangular shaped pieces along the scored lines and leave for at least 2 hours to absorb the syrup. Remove from tin with a spatula. A baklava will keep for up to 1 week in a cool place if covered with cling film or foil.

Preparing Éclairs

Spoon the prepared choux pastry into a piping bag fitted with a 1-cm (½-inch) plain nozzle. Cover a buttered baking tray with greaseproof paper and pipe the pastry into strips about 9cm (3½ inches) long, cut off each length with a knife, allowing about 4cm (1½ inches) between the strips for expansion.

Cook the éclairs in a preheated moderately hot oven (200°C, 400°F, Gas Mark 6) for about 15 minutes. Reduce the oven temperature to moderately hot (190°C, 375°F, Gas Mark 5) and cook for a further 10–15 minutes until well-risen, firm and golden. Pierce the ends of each éclair with a knife to allow any steam to escape. Return to the oven for a further 5 minutes to dry out. Allow to cool on a wire rack. Fill with the chosen filling and ice as liked.

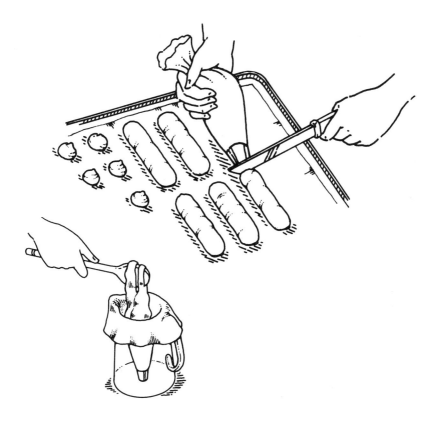

Preparing Profiteroles, Choux Buns or Puffs

Spoon the prepared choux pastry into a piping bag fitted with a 1-cm (½-inch) plain nozzle. This is easiest done if the piping bag is placed in a large jug and the open bag is folded back over the jug rim. Spoon the pastry into the bag and push down to eliminate the air. Either dampen or grease and flour the baking tray and, holding the piping bag in one hand, pipe mounds of the mixture at regular intervals on the tray. Allow plenty of space between each mound for the profiteroles or buns to expand on cooking. When the correct amount of pastry has been squeezed from the bag, cut off with a knife. Alternatively the profiteroles or choux buns can be spooned into mounds on the trays with a wet spoon to aid easy release.

Cook in a preheated hot oven (220°C, 425°F, Gas Mark 7) for 15–20 minutes, according to size, until well-risen, firm to the touch and golden. Remove from the oven and pierce the sides with a knife to allow any steam to escape.

Return to the oven for a further 5 minutes to dry out. Allow to cool on a wire rack. Fill with the chosen filling and ice if liked.

73

Preparing Beignets or Choux Fritters

Choux pastry can form the basis of many delicious sweet or savoury fritters when deep-fried in hot oil. Experiment with sweet choux flavours like orange, lemon, cinnamon or spice and dust with castor sugar to serve, or flavour basic choux with cheese, mustard or bacon and deep fry for a delicious savoury starter dusted with sea salt and a little freshly ground black pepper.

For perfect results, spoon walnut-sized pieces of choux paste into hot oil and cook until crisp and golden brown. The oil should register 180–190°C (350–375°F) on a thermometer or should sizzle when the choux is added. Cook the choux pieces in small batches, so that they do not stick together and have room to expand. Cook for about 5–7 minutes according to size. Drain on absorbent kitchen towel. Always take great care while spooning the choux into the oil to prevent burning.

For a dramatic effect, try piping the choux pastry into the hot oil. Spoon the prepared choux pastry in a piping bag fitted with a small plain or star-shaped nozzle. Pipe small lengths, maximum 7.5 cm (3 inches), into the hot oil, cutting the pastry off near the nozzle with a sharp knife or pair of kitchen scissors. Cook for 5–7 minutes according to size. Drain on absorbent kitchen towel then dust as liked. Serve warm or cold.

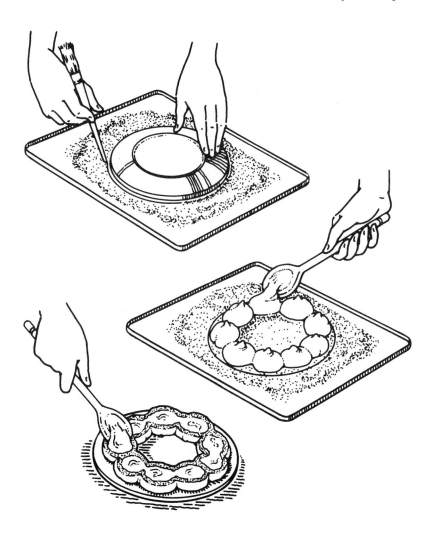

Preparing a Choux Ring

A choux ring using 1 quantity of choux pastry can be made by marking an 18-cm (7-inch) circle on a greased and lightly-floured baking tray. Drop heaped tablespoons of the prepared choux pastry just inside the circle to form a ring; alternatively pipe the choux around the inside of the ring using a large piping bag fitted with a large vegetable nozzle.

Cook in a preheated moderately hot oven (200°C, 400°F, Gas Mark 6) for 40 minutes or until golden and cooked through, or according to specific recipe instructions. Allow to cool slightly then transfer to a wire rack to cool completely. When cold, split the choux ring in half horizontally to fill. Use a teaspoon to scrape out and discard any soft or uncooked pastry inside the ring, leaving a hollow shell. Fill as liked then replace the top.

Preparing a Filet de Boeuf en Croûte or Beef Wellington

Encasing beef in a crisp puff or rough puff pastry is a speciality of the French and perhaps the most classic is Beef Wellington. The instructions given below, however, can be used to prepare any number of different meats or stuffed meats in pastry. For instructions on how to prepare the beef prior to wrapping in pastry see page 139, or specific recipes for other meats.

Roll out the prepared pastry on a lightly-floured surface to about 3mm (⅛ inch) thick and to a rectangle large enough to completely enclose the meat. Place the meat on the centre of the pastry. Brush one long side of the pastry with beaten egg.

Fold the unbrushed side over the meat, fold up the second side and press firmly together. Trim the ends of the pastry at an angle, cutting it straight off close to the meat.

Brush the upper surface of the trimmed ends with beaten egg and fold diagonally across the ends of the parcel, and decorate with pastry trimmings as liked. Leaves are the traditional decoration. Brush again with beaten egg to glaze. Cook according to the specific recipe instructions. (For Filet de Boeuf en Croûte see page 139.)

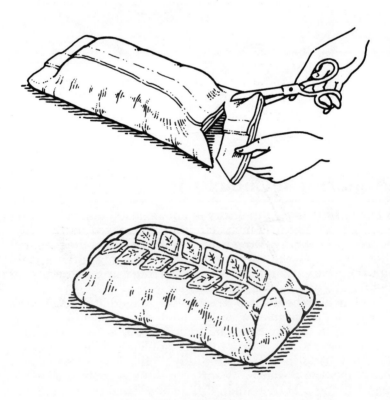

Preparing Danish Pastries

The quantity of Danish pastry (see page 30) will make 16 assorted Danish pastries. To make two of each of the following: windmills, tivolis, spandauers and cocks' combs, roll out half of the prepared pastry on a lightly-floured surface to a rectangle 15 × 30cm (6 × 12 inches). Cut in half lengthwise and then crosswise into quarters to give eight squares each measuring 7.5cm (3 inches).

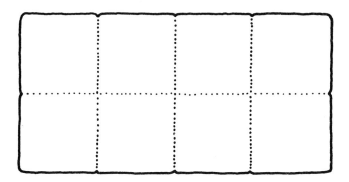

For windmills: Place a little almond paste in the centre of each square and brush lightly around the edge of the square with beaten egg. Make cuts from the corners to within 1cm (½ inch) of the centre. Fold one corner of each cut to the centre to make a windmill and seal with beaten egg.

For tivolis: Place a little apple and raisin filling diagonally across each square then fold the uncovered corners into the centre so that they slightly overlap. Seal with beaten egg white.

For spandauers: Fold each corner from the square of pastry into the centre and press gently to seal. Place a small blob of vanilla cream in the centre. After baking, place a little redcurrant jelly in the centre of each spandauer and drizzle with white glacé icing.

For cocks' combs: Spread the centre of each pastry square with chopped ginger or a glacé fruit mixture and fold over. Seal with a little beaten egg white. With a sharp knife, slash the fold at regular intervals almost to the centre. Brush with egg white and sprinkle with flaked almonds if liked.

To make two cartwheels and snegles divide the remaining pastry in half and roll out, on a lightly-floured surface to a rectangle 30 × 10cm (12 × 4 inches). Cut the pastry lengthwise into two long strips.

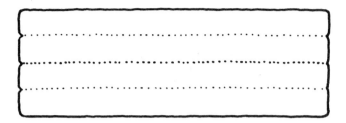

For cartwheels: Spread one of the strips with almond paste and then sprinkle with chopped mixed peel and chopped glacé cherries. Roll up, from the short side, like a Swiss roll. Cut each in half horizontally and cook flat side down. Brush with beaten egg and sprinkle with nuts if liked.

For snegles: Spread the remaining strip with cinnamon sugar and a few currants. Roll up, from the short side, like a Swiss roll. Cut the roll in half horizontally then cut each half nearly all the way through in two places. Open each snegle out like a fan to cook.

Finally to make four **crescents**, roll out the remaining pastry to a 20-cm (8-inch) round and cut into four wedges. Spread each wedge with nuts, cinnamon and sugar, dried fruit, stewed fruit or confectioner's custard and roll up from the wide edge to the point. Curve into a crescent shape to cook.

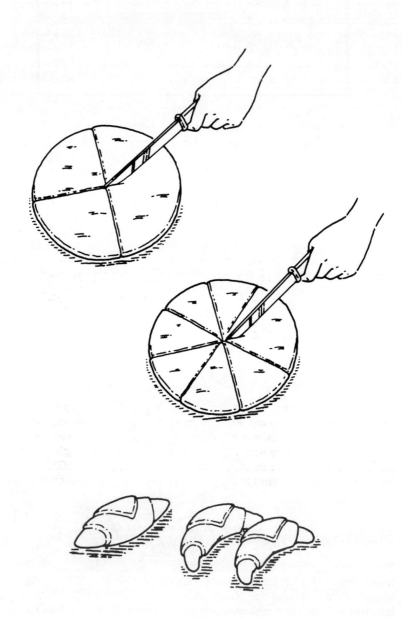

Preparing Brioches

Brush about 20 deep 7.5-cm (3-inch) fluted brioche tins with oil. Divide the prepared brioche dough into about 20 pieces. Cut about a third of the dough away from each piece and set aside. Shape the larger pieces of dough into balls and place in the prepared tins. With a finger, make a hole in the centre of each ball down to the base of the tin. Roll the smaller pieces of dough into balls and place on top of the larger pieces like cottage loaves. Cover with polythene or cling film and leave to rise until they almost reach the tops of the tins. Brush with beaten egg to glaze and cook in a preheated moderately hot oven (200°C, 400°F, Gas Mark 6) for 12–15 minutes.

To make 2 large brioches, brush 2 (1.2-litre/2-pint) fluted brioche moulds with oil. Divide the prepared brioche dough in half. Cut each half into two-third and one-third pieces as before and shape the same way. Brush with beaten egg to glaze and cook in a preheated moderately hot oven (200°C, 400°F, Gas Mark 6) for 20–25 minutes or until golden and cooked through.

Making Christmas Wreaths

To make individual Christmas wreaths, take a heaped teaspoon of the prepared almond pastry and roll into long ropes about 15cm (6 inches) long. Shape each rope into a circle, leaving a 1-cm (½-inch) overlap where the ends cross over each other. Press down gently to seal. Place on greased baking trays

and brush with beaten egg white to glaze. Sprinkle with sugar and decorate with pieces of chopped glacé fruits chosen.

Cook in a preheated moderately hot oven (200°C, 400°F, Gas Mark 6) for 10–12 minutes. Allow to cool on a wire rack.

Preparing Pork Pies or Free-standing Raised Pies

Divide the prepared hot water crust pastry into two-third and one-third portions. Divide each portion into four equal pieces. Roll the larger pieces into 15-cm (6-inch) rounds on a lightly-floured surface. Turn four (450-g/1-lb) jam jars upside down and shape the pastry rounds over their bases. Mould the pastry to give a good shape. Wrap a double piece of greaseproof paper around each of the pastry-lined jars and secure with string. Cover with a tea towel and chill for 2 hours or until firm.

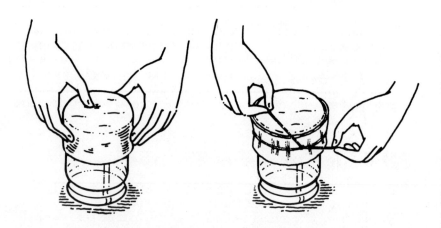

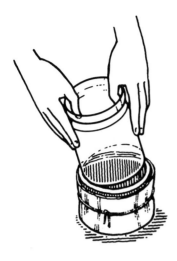
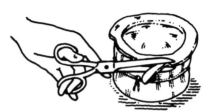

Turn the jars upright and carefully ease the pastry shells away from the jars. Fill with the prepared filling and brush the pastry rim with water.

Roll out the remaining pieces of pastry to make lids for the pies and position on top of the pies. Trim, seal and flute the edges.

Cut a cross in the centre of each pie and fold back the pieces of pastry. Brush with beaten egg to glaze and cook according to specific recipe instructions.

Fill the cooked pies with aspic jelly or jellied stock after cooking.

The same method and amount of pastry can be used to shape a 15-cm (6-inch) free-standing raised pie. Mould the dough over a 15-cm (6-inch) cake tin.

Preparing Cheese or Salted Twisters

Cheese pastry and flavoured shortcrust pastries are ideal to use for these. Roll out the prepared pastry on a lightly-floured surface. Cut into strips each measuring 15 × 2.5cm (6 × 1 inch). Pick up each strip and twist the ends in opposite directions to make twists. Lay them on a greased baking tray, pressing the ends down to prevent curling.

Cook in a preheated hot oven (220°C, 425°F, Gas Mark 7) for 6–8 minutes until golden, or according to the specific recipe instructions. Sprinkle with grated Parmesan cheese, curry powder, seasoned salt, sesame seeds or sea salt as liked. Allow to cool on a wire rack.

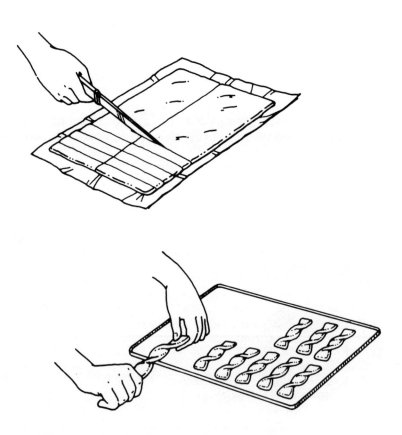

Lining a Tin for a Pastry-lined Pâté

A rich shortcrust pastry is ideal for enclosing a pâté in pastry. You will need about two quantities to line a 20-cm (8-inch) hinged, rectangular raised pie mould.

Roll out three-quarters of the pastry on a lightly-floured surface to a rectangle whose long sides measure slightly more than the mould's length plus twice its height, and the shorter edges measure slightly more than the mould's width plus twice its height.

Lightly grease the mould. Using both hands, lift the pastry and gently ease it into the mould, covering the base and sides evenly. Press the pastry against the base and sides to give a good fit. Trim away any excess pastry.

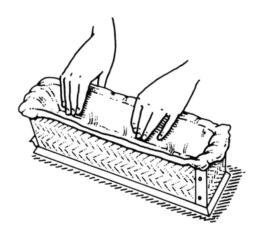

Fill the pastry-lined mould with the chosen filling and brush the pastry edges with beaten egg. Roll out the remaining pastry to make a lid. Position on the mould and seal the edges carefully. Brush with beaten egg to glaze. Decorate the crust with any pastry trimmings if liked and make a small hole in the crust to allow any steam to escape during cooking. Cook according to specific recipe instructions. Unmould to serve. If any aspic or jellied stock is to be used then pour this into the pie through the hole in the crust.

Preparing Cornish Pasties

You will need 1½ quantities of shortcrust pastry to make four pasties. Roll out the prepared pastry on a lightly-floured surface and cut out four (20-cm/8-inch) rounds. Divide the meat and vegetable mixture between the rounds. Dampen the pastry edges with water and draw together to make a seam across the top. Crimp the edges decoratively. Place on a greased baking tray and brush with beaten egg to glaze. Cook in a preheated hot oven (220°C, 425°F, Gas Mark 7) for 15 minutes. Reduce the oven temperature to moderate (160°C, 325°F, Gas Mark 3) and cook for a further 50–60 minutes.

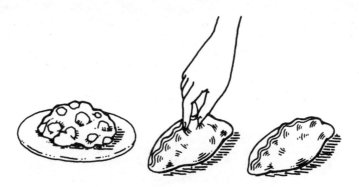

Preparing Turnovers

Roll out the prepared pastry on a lightly-floured surface and cut rounds according to the size of turnover required. You can make turnovers ranging in size from 6–25cm (2¾–10 inches) in diameter for general use. Smaller sizes are ideal for cocktail nibbles whilst larger sizes make good main meal pasties.

Place the filling on one side of the rounds, taking care not to overfill the turnovers. Dampen the pastry edges with water or beaten egg and fold the pastry over the filling. Seal the edges with a fork or flute decoratively. Place on a greased or dampened baking tray according to pastry type and brush with beaten egg to glaze. Cook according to specific recipe instructions.

To Make Phyllo Pastry Tricorns

Cut sheets of prepared phyllo pastry into 7.5cm (3 inch) wide strips and brush with melted butter. Place a small teaspoon of the chosen filling in the bottom corner of the strip. Fold the phyllo pastry over the filling to make a triangle. Continue folding the pastry over the filling, but keeping the triangular shape. Brush again with butter and cook according to specific recipe instructions. As a guideline most tricorns made with phyllo pastry are cooked in a preheated moderately hot oven (190°C, 375°F, Gas Mark 5) for about 20 minutes.

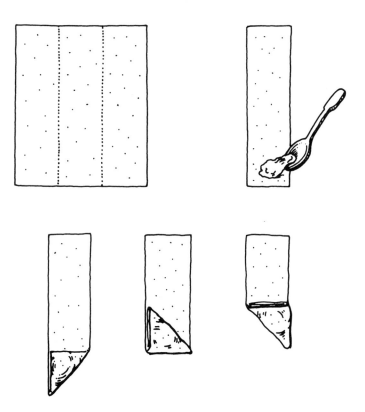

THE FINISHING TOUCH

... pastry decorations to be proud of

Even if your pastry is delicious and has a fine reputation it can let you down if visually it doesn't come up to scratch. Interesting edges, cleverly cut-out decorations and shiny glazes will all help to lift pastry from the ordinary to the luxury class. Start first by trimming, knocking-up and fluting the edges like the experts then let your imagination take over with ideas for pastry decorations that are truly individual:

Trimming and 'knocking-up' the edges
Trim the pastry edges with a sharp knife taking care to get a clean and even cut. It is then essential to seal the edges firmly together by 'knocking-up'. To do this, hold the knife in a horizontal position with the edge and with your index finger pressed firmly along the inner rim, tap the pastry edge firmly with the blunt side of the blade to give a rippled, flaky effect. The edge can then be decorated in a number of ways:

Fluting and scalloping the edges
Flute or scallop the edges by pressing down with the thumb and forefinger to make scallops at intervals while at the same time cutting the edge lightly with the back of a knife, pulling up vertically. Traditionally sweet pies have smaller flutes or scallops around their rims than savoury pies.

Making a daisy edge
A decorative daisy edge can be produced on the rim of a pie, tart or flan by pressing around the pastry edge with the handle of a teaspoon.

Crimping the edges
To crimp the edges of a pie, push the thumb and first finger of one hand into the pastry rim. With the thumb of the second hand, pinch the pastry between the fingers to give a crimped effect.

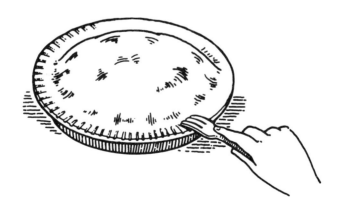

Forking the edges
To give a forked effect on the edge of a pie or flan, press a floured fork around the outer edge of the pastry rim.

Roping the edges

To give a roped edge to a pie or pastry, press your thumb into the pastry edge at an angle and pinch the pastry between it and the knuckle of your index finger. Repeat this all the way around the edge, remembering to place your thumb each time in the indentation made by the index finger.

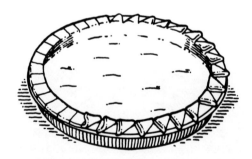

Decorative cutting of the edges

There are an infinite number of ways in which you can cut the edges of pastry to give an attractive edge. A folded cut-edge is one of the most popular. Make small cuts about 1cm (½ inch) deep at 1-cm (½-inch) intervals around the pastry edge. Fold in alternate cuts and press down firmly to secure.

A triangular cut-edge is made by cutting the rim of the pastry at 1-cm (½-inch) intervals. Brush with water then fold each piece of pastry over to form a triangle.

Plaiting or twisting the edges

Roll out any pastry trimmings on a lightly-floured surface and cut into long thin strips. Twist or plait these together. Dampen the pastry rim with water and attach the plait or twist pressing down lightly to seal.

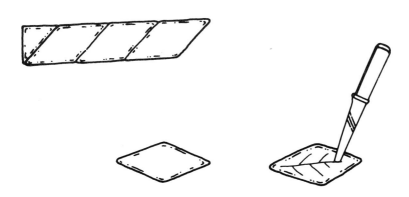

Making pastry leaves

To make pastry leaves, roll out any pastry trimmings on a lightly-floured surface and cut into strips. Cut the strips diagonally to form diamond shapes. Mark the 'veins' with the back of a knife. Dampen lightly with water before fixing to the pastry dish.

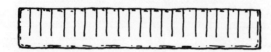

Making a pastry tassel

To make a pastry tassel, roll out any pastry trimmings on a lightly-floured surface and cut a strip 2.5 × 15cm (1 × 6 inches). Make 2-cm (¾-inch) cuts at narrow intervals along the strip. Roll up from the short end like a Swiss roll and place on the main dish. Carefully fan out the cuts to form a tassel.

Making pastry roses

To make pastry roses, roll out any pastry trimmings on a lightly-floured surface and stamp out 4-cm (1½-inch) rounds. Cut each round in half and brush with a little beaten egg. With the straight edge as a base, roll up one half to form the centre. Wrap the second half around the first carefully concealing the join. Continue with further semi-circles until the rose is complete.

Making pastry fruit, fish and flower shapes
Almost any number of different shapes can be cut out of pastry to decorate pies, flans and tarts. Fruit, fish and flowers are obvious choices for fruit-filled, fish-filled and fragrant smelling dishes. Experiment too with cut-out letters to reveal the pie filling and use other shapes like stars, hearts, moons and triangles to give an attractive pie decoration.

Making a pastry lattice
One of the most attractive ways to decorate an open tart is to make a pastry lattice. Roll out any pastry trimmings on a lightly-floured surface and cut into narrow strips about 1cm (½ inch) wide. Twist if liked, then arrange half the strips at regular intervals across the filling one way then place the remaining strips at right angles to the first. Trim the ends and dampen with a little water to seal to the pastry rim.

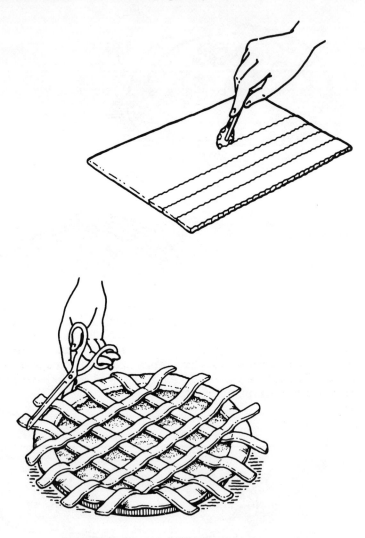

To prepare an interwoven lattice, fold back alternate strips of the first lattice of strips and add the second batch of strips at right angles. Replace the folded back strips and lift back the alternate ones and continue until complete.

Making a leaf or circular edging
Roll out any pastry trimmings on a lightly-floured surface and cut into pastry leaves or 2-cm (¾-inch) circles with a small cutter. Dampen the pastry rim with water and arrange the leaves just overlapping each other around the edge of the pie crust, alternatively arrange the pastry circles just overlapping each other around the pastry rim.

PASTRY MAKING AND BAKING EQUIPMENT

It may seem ironic, that living in a technologically-conscious world, the most important tools required for good pastry making are your hands. Specialist tools will often help make a job easier and sometimes will efficiently dispense with the need for hands but generally these are all that you require in the realms of basic tools for successful pastry making. Mixing, blending, shaping and decorating can all be performed with relative ease. Success or failure in these tasks will generally depend upon the temperature of your hands. Cool hands are ideal for rubbing fat into flour for shortcrust type pastries, while warm hands are invaluable for kneading and pounding a bread-type dough. Strength is an asset for pounding and softening butter when preparing pâte sucrée yet delicate precision is welcome when crimping or decorating a pastry pie crust. No one tool can perform all of these tasks as efficiently as the hands. There are however, a whole host of tools which do help with pastry making from the basic rolling pin to the sophisticated pastry blender which you may find useful.

Knives
If you have a good selection of kitchen knives in your kitchen then you are bound to find the ideal one for the vast number of tasks performed in pastry making with a knife. As a general rule a good sharp knife that is comfortable to hold is the ideal companion. Choose a straight, firm knife that will cut through the pastry neatly – dragging the dough will only result in uneven rising and give an untidy end result. Use the back of a knife for 'knocking-up' the edges of the dough and the point for any scoring work.

A palette knife is useful for spreading pastry fillings evenly and one with a serrated edge is excellent for cutting and serving flans and quiches. A palette knife will also prove useful for lifting pastries from their baking trays.

Pastry and Dough Scrapers
There is a good selection of pastry and dough scrapers on the market ranging from the rigid metal type that look similar to the type you use in painting and decorating to the flexible plastic ones that icing specialists use. Rigid spatulas are ideal for mixing ingredients and also for cleaning work surfaces clear of pastry trimmings. Flexible spatulas are ideal for mixing pastries that use the 'well' method.

Weighing Scales

Scales are an absolute must in ensuring that ingredients are in the correct proportions. Always follow one set of measures, Imperial or metric, since the quantities are not interchangeable.

Measuring Spoons

Measuring spoons are just as important as scales in measuring ingredients. Choose a set that has a good range of sizes. Imperial spoons usually include ¼, ½ and 1 teaspoon measures with a 1 tablespoon measure. A metric set will include 2.5, 5, 10 and 15ml spoons.

Marble and Other Work Surfaces

Marble is the ideal work top for making pastry since it keeps cool during the mixing and folding processes. If you do not have a marble slab then any clean, dry work surface will usually suffice.

Pastry Brushes

A good selection of pastry brushes of varying sizes will prove invaluable for glazing pastries and tarts prior to baking. Smaller brushes are ideal for delicate decorative pieces and a larger one for larger surface coating. Use the larger flat type of pastry brush for glazing vast areas and the round-shaped brush for decorations since it will reach into the tiniest of crevices. Both flat and round will cope admirably with glazes for pastry tarts. If you want to put the lightest of egg white glazes on a pastry then use the specialist old fashioned goose feather brush.

Sieves

A sieve will prove very useful in quickly and efficiently sifting flour with any other seasonings, flavourings or raising agents. A plastic sieve will often prove the easiest to clean. A sturdier metal type sieve will prove useful in puréeing fruit fillings and sieving glazes prior to use.

Measuring Jugs

A good selection will prove a worthwhile investment. Choose a variety of sizes from 300ml (½ pint), 600ml (1 pint) and 1 litre (1¾ pint) for eye level accuracy.

Flour Dredgers

A flour dredger is a must for even sprinkling of flour over both work surface and rolling pin. It is also the foolproof way of making sure that you do not add too much flour with a heavy hand. There are a vast array available from metal, pottery, glass and china. Don't just use it for flour, it will prove useful for sprinkling sugar and spices over pies and tarts.

Pastry Wheels

Fluted pastry wheels are available for cutting decorative strips of pastry to use on tarts, pies and other pastry dishes. Alongside them come pastry trimmers which ensure a good clean cut to a pie edge. An ingenious device which cuts a pie edge and decorates it too is also available for those who really haven't the time for a hand finished job.

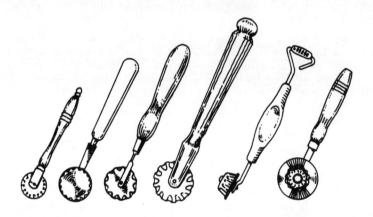

Baking Trays

A large variety will prove useful in coping with large pastries to small cocktail nibbles. A large flat tray is a good investment alongside a few with raised edges if juices might leak out. Always buy the best quality you can afford since it will have endless uses in pastry making from holding pizzas, shortbread, jalousies, pastry shapes and biscuits and will also act as a base for flan rings and bottomless frames. A baking tray is also useful when cooking pastries in ceramic dishes - a ceramic dish should be placed on a metal tray so that the heat is conducted more evenly to the base of the dish.

Baking Beans

If you frequently bake tart and flan cases blind, then a supply of baking beans could prove useful. Either set aside a quantity of dried peas or beans for this use or invest in a set of ceramic baking beans available in specialist kitchen supply shops.

Flan Cases and Rings

These are available with bases or without, fluted or plain and in a large number of sizes from about 10cm (4 inches) in diameter to 30cm (12 inches) in diameter for regular use. Ceramic flan cases or china flan cases can make an attractive dish for serving pastries as well as cooking them - use ceramic dishes in conjunction with metal baking trays for best results.

98

Cooling Rack
A wire cooling rack is essential for cooling and crisping small and large pastries. Choose a large all-purpose one for maximum use.

Pie Funnels
A pie funnel will prove invaluable if the pie filling is moist and likely to make a pastry crust soggy. Choose one that is tall enough to stand above the pastry rim allowing any steam to make its way efficiently through the crust.

Pie Plates
A wide selection will give variety from shallow to deep. A metal pie plate will give good cooking results. If using a glass or ceramic pie plate then stand it on a metal baking tray during cooking.

Patty Tins
The selection you choose here will depend upon how often you cook small pastries like open tarts, double-crust individual pies to larger hot water crust pork pies. Always choose those made from a good quality metal and of sturdy design.

Spring Form Tins
Spring form tins prove infinitely useful when making pastry lined cheesecakes and flans of a delicate nature. They efficiently and neatly ensure a clean release from the baking tin.

Pastry Cutters
Whatever the shape there is almost always a cutter available for it. Round fluted and plain pastry cutters are probably the only ones you will really need frequently but you can choose from cocktail cutters, alphabet cutters, heart-shaped cutters, fruit-shaped cutters, fish-shaped cutters, aspic cutters, vol-au-vent cutters both round and square, triangular cutters etc.

Piping Bags and Nozzles
Piping bags and nozzles will be required for piping the softer pastry pastes like choux. A selection of sizes and shapes will prove a good investment. Choose piping bags that are easy to clean.

Cling Film, Polythene and Foil
These are all useful in covering, wrapping and baking procedures for pastry. Wrap pastry while chilling in polythene, cling film or foil. Bake pastries 'blind' using greaseproof paper or foil and beans. Freeze pastries in a freezer type polythene or foil for good storage and cover yeasted pastries with cling film during the rising and proving processes.

Specialist Baking Tins

Special tins for baking raised pies, pastry loaves, special shaped pies, tranches, brioches, boat-shaped pastries, cream horns and other small pastries are all available from specialist kitchen shops.

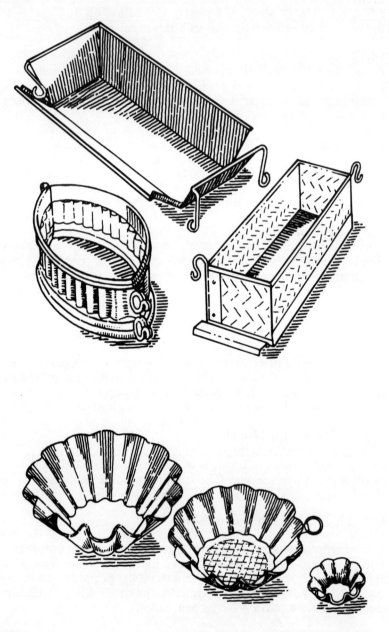

Rolling Pin

Choose a rolling pin that is long, even and without ridges for good overall use. Cool pins are also available for especially rolling out pastry – these are usually made of china, marble or glass and some are hollow to hold iced water. Lightly flour rolling pins before rolling out pastry and clean after use with a damp cloth.

Your rolling pin will find a multitude of other uses too – it will help in lifting pastry over pies and flans, in shaping pastry type biscuits before and after cooking, in crushing biscuits and crumbs for cheesecake bases and in giving a good clean cut edge to flans and tartlet moulds.

RECIPE SECTION

SMALL SAVOURY PASTRIES AND COCKTAIL NIBBLES

Gammon and Sweetcorn Puffs

Serves 4

15g (½ oz) butter
1 small onion, peeled and
  chopped
1 (227-g/8-oz) can peeled
  tomatoes, drained and
  chopped
½ teaspoon Worcestershire
  sauce
1 teaspoon cornflour
100g (4 oz) canned sweetcorn
  with peppers

100g (4 oz) cooked gammon,
  coarsely chopped
salt and freshly ground black
  pepper
½ quantity Puff Pastry
  (see page 25)
beaten egg to glaze
sesame seeds
  to sprinkle

Melt the butter in a saucepan. Add the onion and cook for 2–3 minutes. Add the tomatoes and Worcestershire sauce and cook for a further 5 minutes. Mix the cornflour with a little water and stir into the tomato mixture. Cook, stirring constantly, until thickened. Add the sweetcorn and gammon and mix well. Season to taste and leave until cold.

Roll out the prepared pastry on a lightly-floured surface and cut into four (13-cm/5-inch) squares. Divide the filling into four. Place a portion on each of the pastry squares. Brush the edges with beaten egg and fold over to completely enclose, making triangular pastries, sealing well.

Place on a dampened baking tray and brush with beaten egg to glaze. Sprinkle with sesame seeds and cook in a preheated hot oven (220°C, 425°F, Gas Mark 7) for 20–25 minutes until well-risen, golden brown and cooked through. Serve hot.

Italian Picnic Pasties

Serves 6

1½ quantities Shortcrust
  Pastry (see page 12)
1 (198-g/7-oz) can tuna in oil
225g (8 oz) leeks, sliced
1 tablespoon flour
1 (450-g/15-oz) can baked
  beans in tomato sauce

½ teaspoon mixed dried herbs
grated rind of ½ lemon
salt and freshly ground black
  pepper
1 egg, beaten

Roll out the prepared pastry on a lightly-floured surface and cut out six (18-cm/7-inch) rounds.

Meanwhile, drain the oil from the tuna into a saucepan. Add

the leeks and sauté until soft. Add the flour and cook for 1 minute. Add the baked beans and simmer for 2 minutes. Remove from the heat and add the flaked tuna, herbs, lemon rind and seasoning to taste. Allow to cool.

Spoon the filling onto one half of each pastry round. Brush the edges with beaten egg and fold the pastry over to completely enclose and encase the filling. Seal and flute the edges and cook in a preheated moderately hot oven (200°C, 400°F, Gas Mark 6) for 25–30 minutes until cooked and golden brown. Allow to cool on a wire rack. Serve the pasties with crisps and salad vegetables.

Pork and Apricot Patties

Makes 12

15g (½ oz) butter
1 onion, peeled and finely chopped
350g (12 oz) lean pork, chopped
175g (6 oz) fresh apricots, peeled, stoned and chopped or 1 small can apricots in natural juices, drained and chopped
1 teaspoon finely chopped fresh sage
salt and freshly ground black pepper
1 quantity Wholemeal Shortcrust Pastry (see page 12)
beaten egg to glaze

Melt the butter in a saucepan. Add the onion and pork and sauté over a high heat until lightly browned. Add the apricots, sage and seasoning to taste. Allow to cool.

Roll out the prepared pastry on a lightly-floured surface and cut out twelve round bases and twelve lids to fit twelve patty tins. Fit the bases into the patty tins (see page 58). Divide the filling into twelve equal portions and place in the patty tins. Dampen the pastry edges with water and cover with the lids, sealing well.

Brush with beaten egg to glaze and cook in a preheated moderately hot oven (200°C, 400°F, Gas Mark 6) for about 30 minutes until golden and cooked through. Serve hot or cold.

Chicken Veronique vol-au-vents

Serves 4

*¼ quantity Puff Pastry (see
  page 25)
beaten egg to glaze
25g (1 oz) butter
25g (1 oz) flour
300ml (½ pint) chicken stock*

*150ml (¼ pint) double cream
350g (12 oz) cooked chicken
  meat, chopped
250g (9 oz) green grapes,
  halved and seeded*

Roll out the prepared pastry on a lightly-floured surface to about
1cm (½ inch) thickness and cut out four (13-cm/5-inch) vol-au-
vents (see page 61). Brush with beaten egg to glaze and cook in a
preheated hot oven (220°C, 425°F, Gas Mark 7) for 10 minutes
until golden. Remove the lids from the bases with a sharp knife
and scoop out any soft pastry from the insides of the vol-au-vents
and discard. Cool the bases and lids on a wire rack.

Meanwhile, melt the butter in a saucepan. Add the flour and
cook for 2–3 minutes or until straw-coloured. Gradually add the
stock, stirring to make a smooth sauce. Add the cream, bring to
the boil and simmer until smooth. Add the chicken and grapes
and toss lightly in the sauce.

Return the vol-au-vent lids and bases to the oven and heat
through for 5 minutes. Spoon the chicken and grape mixture into
the vol-au-vent cases and top with the lids. Serve at once.

Sesame and Sausage Rolls

Makes about 20

*1 quantity Shortcrust Pastry
  (see page 12)
275g (10 oz) sausagemeat
salt and freshly ground black
  pepper*

*flour to dust
beaten egg to glaze
2 tablespoons sesame seeds*

Roll out the prepared pastry on a lightly-floured surface to a
large rectangle. Mix the sausagemeat with seasoning to taste
and divide into two equal pieces. Roll each into a long sausage
the length of the pastry rectangle. Cut the pastry rectangle in
half lengthways. Lay a sausagemeat roll down the length of
each pastry strip. Dampen the pastry edges with water and fold
one side of each strip of pastry over the sausagemeat filling and
press firmly together to seal. Knock up the edges with a sharp
knife then cut the rolls into smaller rolls about 4–5cm (1½–2
inches) long. Place on a dampened baking tray.

Brush the sausage rolls with beaten egg to glaze and sprinkle with the sesame seeds. Cook in a preheated moderately hot oven (200°C, 400°F, Gas Mark 6) for 15 minutes. Reduce the oven temperature to moderate (180°C, 350°F, Gas Mark 4) and cook for a further 15 minutes.

Bacon and Crab Whirls

Makes 24

225g (8 oz) streaky bacon, rinds removed and finely chopped
100g (4 oz) button mushrooms, finely chopped
1 (42-g / 1½-oz) can dressed crab

salt and freshly ground black pepper
½ quantity Puff Pastry (see page 25

Mix the bacon with the mushrooms, crab and seasoning to taste.

Roll out the prepared pastry on a lightly-floured surface to a rectangle 30 × 20cm (12 × 8 inches). Spread the filling evenly over the pastry then roll up carefully lengthwise. Using a sharp knife, carefully cut the roll into 1-cm (½-inch) slices.

Place on dampened baking tray, about 2.5cm (1 inch) apart. Cook in a preheated hot oven (230°C, 450°F, Gas Mark 8) for 15–20 minutes. Serve hot or cold.

Stilton and Sausagemeat Nibbles

Makes 18

*½ quantity Puff Pastry (see
    page 25)*
50g (2 oz) Stilton cheese
*4 teaspoons made English
    mustard*

100g (4 oz) sausagemeat
*salt and freshly ground black
    pepper*
beaten egg to glaze

Roll out the prepared pastry on a lightly-floured surface and cut
out eighteen (5-cm/2-inch) rounds with a fluted biscuit cutter.

Mix the cheese with the mustard, sausagemeat and seasoning to
taste. Place a small amount of filling in the centre of each round.
Brush the edges with beaten egg, fold the pastry over and crimp
together to form small crescents.

Place on a dampened baking tray and brush with beaten egg to
glaze. Cook in a preheated moderately hot oven (200°C, 400°F,
Gas Mark 6) for 10 minutes. Reduce the oven temperature to
moderate (180°C, 350°F, Gas Mark 4) and cook for a further 10
minutes. Serve hot with drinks.

York Bacon Triangles

Serves 4-5

15g (½ oz) butter
*1 small onion, peeled and
    finely chopped*
*100g (4 oz) smoked back bacon,
    rinds removed and chopped*
*50g (2 oz) Cheddar cheese,
    grated*

freshly ground black pepper
*¼ quantity Puff Pastry (see
    page 25)*
*made English mustard to
    spread*
beaten egg to glaze

Melt the butter in a saucepan. Add the onion and bacon and
sauté until golden, about 8-10 minutes. Allow to cool slightly
and stir in the cheese and freshly ground black pepper to taste.

Roll out the prepared pastry on a lightly-floured surface and
cut out ten to twelve (7.5-cm/3-inch) rounds. Spread each round
with a little mustard. Spoon a small amount of filling onto each
round. Brush the pastry edges with beaten egg and fold up to
make tricorn shapes (see page 87).

Place on a dampened baking tray and brush with beaten egg to
glaze. Cook in a preheated moderately hot oven (200°C, 400°F,
Gas Mark 6) for 10-15 minutes until well-risen, golden brown
and cooked through. Serve warm or cold.

Danish Cheese and Bacon Tricorns

Makes 8

15g (½ oz) butter
1 small onion, peeled and
 finely chopped
75g (3 oz) streaky bacon,
 rinds removed and chopped
50g (2 oz) Samso cheese,
 grated

freshly ground black pepper
1 tablespoon tomato purée
¼ quantity Puff Pastry (see
 page 25)
beaten egg to glaze

Melt the butter in a saucepan. Add the onion and bacon and sauté until golden, about 8–10 minutes. Allow to cool slightly and stir in the cheese, ground black pepper to taste and tomato purée.

Roll out the prepared pastry on a lightly-floured surface and cut out eight (10-cm/4-inch) rounds. Spoon a small amount of filling onto each round. Brush the pastry edges with beaten egg and fold up to make tricorn shapes (see page 87).

Place on a dampened baking tray and brush with beaten egg to glaze. Cook in a preheated moderately hot oven (200°C, 400°F, Gas Mark 6) for 15 minutes until well-risen, golden brown and cooked through. Serve warm or cold.

Cheese Fleurons

Makes 18

½ quantity Puff Pastry (see
 page 25)
beaten egg to glaze
50g (2 oz) Red Leicester cheese,
 grated

2 tablespoons grated
 Parmesan cheese

Roll out the prepared pastry on a lightly-floured surface and cut out eighteen (8.5-cm/3½-inch) rounds using a fluted biscuit or scone cutter. Fold over each round to produce semi-circle shapes or fleurons and press well together (see page 86). Chill for about 15 minutes.

Place on dampened baking trays and sprinkle with the Red Leicester and Parmesan cheeses. Cook in a preheated hot oven (220°C, 425°F, Gas Mark 7) for 20 minutes until well-risen, crisp and golden brown. Serve hot with casseroles or with drinks.

Cheese and Mustard Fingers

Makes about 80

225g (8 oz) plain flour
pinch of salt
2 teaspoons dry mustard
  powder
100g (4 oz) butter
3–4 tablespoons cold water

2 tablespoons made American
  mustard
175g (6 oz) Lancashire cheese,
  grated
beaten egg to glaze

Sift the flour, salt and mustard powder into a mixing bowl. Cut the butter into small pieces and rub into the flour until the mixture resembles fine breadcrumbs. Bind to a stiff but manageable dough with the water. Chill for 10 minutes.

Roll out the pastry on a lightly-floured surface to a rectangle about 3mm (⅛ inch) thick. Spread the pastry with one-third of the American mustard. Sprinkle 50g (2 oz) of the Lancashire cheese over the pastry. Fold the pastry into three. Give the pastry a half turn and roll out again to 3mm (⅛ inch) thick. Repeat the process twice, spreading with the mustard and sprinkling with the cheese as before. Chill for 10 minutes.

Roll out the pastry to a rectangle about 3mm (⅛ inch) thick and cut into sticks measuring 1 × 7.5cm (½ × 3 inches). Place on greased baking trays and brush with beaten egg to glaze. Cook in a preheated moderately hot oven (200°C, 400°F, Gas Mark 6) for 15 minutes until golden brown. Allow to cool on a wire rack. Store in an airtight tin until required.

Crab and Apple Puffs

Makes 10

1 quantity Herby Shortcrust
  Pastry (see page 13)
100g (4 oz) flaked crab meat
1 eating or dessert apple,
  peeled, cored and grated

2 tablespoons double cream
salt and freshly ground black
  pepper
oil for deep frying
sea salt crystals to serve

Roll out the prepared pastry on a lightly-floured surface and cut out twenty rounds with a 5-cm (2-inch) fluted scone or biscuit cutter.

Mix the crab meat with the apple, double cream and seasoning to taste. Place a little of the filling on half of the rounds. Dampen the pastry edges with water and top with the remaining rounds, pinching together to seal well.

Heat the oil to 180°C (350°F). Deep fry the puffs in the hot oil until golden brown and puffy, about 5 minutes. Drain on absorbent kitchen towel. Toss in sea salt crystals to serve.

Gruyère and Mushroom Puffs

Makes 6

1 quantity Choux Pastry (see
   page 34)
25g (1 oz) butter
50g (2 oz) mushrooms, sliced
3 tablespoons flour
1 teaspoon made tarragon
   mustard

300ml (½ pint) milk
100g (4 oz) Gruyère cheese,
   grated
salt and freshly ground black
   pepper
6 rashers streaky bacon, rinds
   removed

Spoon the prepared pastry in a piping bag fitted with a 1-cm (½-inch) plain nozzle. Pipe six éclairs onto a baking tray each about 10cm (4 inches) long (see page 72). Cook in a preheated moderately hot oven (200°C, 400°F, Gas Mark 6) for 40 minutes. Remove from the oven and slit along the sides to allow any steam to escape. Return to the oven for a further 5 minutes to dry out.

Meanwhile, melt the butter in a pan. Add the mushrooms and sauté until lightly coloured. Stir in the flour and mustard and cook for 1 minute. Gradually add the milk and cook to make a thick sauce, stirring. Add half of the cheese and seasoning to taste. Fill the éclairs with the cheese mixture. Stretch the bacon rashers with the back of a knife and wrap a rasher around each éclair. Place on a baking tray and sprinkle with the remaining cheese.

Increase the oven temperature to hot (220°C, 425°F, Gas Mark 7) and cook the éclairs for 10-15 minutes until the bacon is crisp and golden. Serve at once.

Cheese Twisters

Makes about 50

1 quantity Basic Cheese
   Pastry (see page 16)

grated Parmesan cheese or
   sea salt to sprinkle

Roll out the prepared pastry on a lightly-floured surface and cuts into strips, each measuring 15 × 2.5cm (6 × 1 inch). Pick up each strip and twist the ends in opposite directions to make twists. Place on greased baking trays, pressing the ends down to prevent them from curling (see page 84).

Cook in a preheated hot oven (220°C, 425°F, Gas Mark 7) for 6-8 minutes until golden. While still hot, sprinkle with grated Parmesan cheese or sea salt. Allow to cool slightly then transfer to a wire rack to cool completely.

Hot Savoury Puffs

Makes 21

*¼ quantity Puff Pastry (see
    page 25)*
milk to glaze
FILLING
300ml (½ pint) béchamel sauce
*1 tablespoon made French
    mustard*

*1 (130-g/4½-oz) can crab meat,
    drained*
*75g (3 oz) blue Stilton cheese,
    crumbled*
*4 rashers streaky bacon,
    cooked and crumbled*

Roll out the prepared pastry on a lightly-floured surface to a rectangle 35 × 30cm (14 × 12 inches). Using a sharp knife, cut the pastry into seven strips 5cm (2 inches) wide. Cut each strip into 5cm (2 inch) long diagonals and place on a dampened baking tray. Brush with milk to glaze and cook in a preheated hot oven (220°C, 425°F, Gas Mark 7) for 10 minutes until golden.

Meanwhile blend the béchamel sauce with the mustard. Divide the sauce into three portions. Mix one portion with the crabmeat, a second portion with the Stilton and the final portion with the bacon. Sandwich the fillings between two puff pastry diagonals, making seven of each flavour. Warm gently in the oven for a few minutes before serving.

Greek Cheese Tricorns

Makes 40

225g (8 oz) cream cheese
100g (4 oz) feta cheese
*100g (4 oz) Gruyère cheese,
    grated*
1 egg

*3 tablespoons chopped fresh
    parsley*
*10 sheets Phyllo Pastry (see
    page 41)*
225g (8 oz) butter, melted

Place the cream cheese and feta cheese in a blender and liquidise until smooth. Remove to a bowl. Add the Gruyère cheese, egg and parsley, and beat well to combine.

Place one sheet of the prepared pastry on a board and brush with a little of the melted butter. Cut the pastry into 7.5-cm (3-inch) strips. Place a heaped teaspoon of the filling in the lower corner of the strip, then fold the phyllo pastry over the filling to make a triangle. Continue folding the strip of pastry over the filling, but keeping the triangular shape (see page 87). Place each completed triangle on greased baking trays. Continue to shape more tricorns with the remaining pastry and filling. Brush the tricorns with melted butter.

Cook in a preheated moderately hot oven (190°C, 375°F, Gas Mark 5) for 20 minutes until golden and puffed. Serve warm.

Chicken and Mushroom Bouchées

Makes about 12

¼ quantity Puff Pastry (see
page 25)
beaten egg to glaze
2 chicken breasts, coarsely
minced
50g (2 oz) butter
25g (1 oz) mushrooms, sliced

90ml (3 fl oz) Noilly Prat or dry
white Vermouth
150ml (¼ pint) double cream
100g (4 oz) Double Gloucester
cheese, grated
salt and freshly ground black
pepper

Roll out the prepared pastry on a lightly-floured surface to about 1cm (½ inch) thickness and cut out about twelve (7.5-cm/ 3-inch) vol-au-vents (see page 61). Brush with beaten egg to glaze and cook in a preheated hot oven (220°C, 425°F, Gas Mark 7) for 10 minutes until golden. Remove the lids from the bases with a sharp knife and scoop out any soft pastry from the insides of the vol-au-vents and discard. Keep warm.

Meanwhile, melt the butter in a saucepan. Add the chicken and cook for about 5 minutes. Remove with a slotted spoon. Add the mushrooms and cook for 1 minute. Remove the mushrooms with a slotted spoon and add the Noilly Prat to the pan juices. Cook over a high heat until reduced by about half. Add the double cream and three-quarters of the cheese. Heat gently until smooth and creamy. Remove from the heat and add the chicken and mushrooms. Season to taste and spoon into the bouchée cases. Sprinkle with the remaining cheese, replace the tops and serve.

SAVOURY QUICHES, TARTS AND FLANS

Spinach and Saint Paulin Flan

Serves 6

PASTRY
175g (6 oz) plain flour
pinch of salt
40g (1½ oz) butter
75g (3 oz) cream cheese
2 tablespoons milk
FILLING
1 tablespoon oil
1 clove garlic, peeled and
  minced
1 small onion, peeled and
  chopped

1 (398-g/14-oz) can peeled
  tomatoes
4 teaspoons tomato purée
salt and freshly ground black
  pepper
450g (1 lb) spinach, cooked and
  very finely chopped
2 tablespoons double cream
pinch of ground nutmeg
175g (6 oz) piece Saint Paulin
  cheese, rind removed

Prepare the pastry: sift the flour with the salt. Beat the butter and cream cheese together until light and fluffy. Gradually add the flour and milk, and bind to make a firm but pliable dough. Wrap in greaseproof paper or cling film and chill for 30 minutes.

Roll out the pastry on a lightly-floured surface and use to line a 20-cm (8-inch) flan ring on a greased baking tray (see page 54). Prick the base well with a fork and bake 'blind' in a preheated moderately hot oven (200°C, 400°F, Gas Mark 6) for 15 minutes (see page 54). Remove the foil or beans and cook for a further 5 minutes.

Prepare the filling: heat the oil in a saucepan. Add the garlic and cook for 2–3 minutes. Add the onion and cook for a further 2 minutes. Add the tomatoes and their juice, tomato purée and seasoning to taste. Boil rapidly for 8 minutes until reduced to a thick paste.

Place the spinach in another saucepan and reheat gently. Add the cream and nutmeg. Spoon the tomato mixture into the pastry case. Top with the spinach mixture. Slice the cheese thinly and arrange decoratively on top of the flan. Reduce the oven temperature to moderate (180°C, 350°F, Gas Mark 4) and cook the flan for 6–10 minutes until warmed through. Serve warm, cut into wedges.

Creamy Cheese and Prawn Flan

Serves 6

PASTRY
175g (6 oz) plain flour
pinch of salt
1 teaspoon dry mustard powder
100g (4 oz) butter
50g (2 oz) grated Parmesan
  cheese
cold water to bind

FILLING
15g (½ oz) butter
1 small onion, peeled and
  finely chopped

3 large (size 1, 2) eggs, beaten
100g (4 oz) shelled prawns
150ml (¼ pint) single cream
salt and freshly ground black
  pepper
2 teaspoons dry mustard
  powder
tomato and cucumber slices to
  garnish

Prepare the pastry: sift the flour with the salt and mustard into a mixing bowl. Cut the butter into small pieces and rub into the flour until the mixture resembles fine breadcrumbs. Add the Parmesan cheese, mixing well. Bind to a firm but pliable dough with cold water.

Roll out the pastry on a lightly-floured surface and use to line a 23-cm (9-inch) flan ring or oval flan dish (see page 54). Bake 'blind' in a preheated hot oven (220°C, 425°F, Gas Mark 7) for 12–15 minutes (see page 54). Remove the foil or beans.

Prepare the filling: melt the butter in a saucepan. Add the onion and fry until softened, about 5–8 minutes. Allow to cool slightly, add the eggs, prawns, cream, seasoning to taste and mustard. Pour into the pastry case and cook in a preheated moderate oven (180°C, 350°F, Gas Mark 4) for about 20–30 minutes until just set. Serve hot or cold, garnished with tomato and cucumber slices.

Mushroom and Marjoram Flans

Makes 6

PASTRY
75g (3 oz) plain wholewheat
  flour
75g (3 oz) plain flour
pinch of salt
75g (3 oz) butter
3 tablespoons cold water

FILLING
2 tablespoons oil

225g (8 oz) button mushrooms
1 small onion, peeled and
  chopped
2 eggs
150ml (¼ pint) single cream
1 teaspoon chopped fresh
  marjoram
salt and freshly ground black
  pepper

Prepare the pastry: mix the flours and salt in a mixing bowl. Cut the butter into small pieces and rub into the flour until the mixture resembles fine breadcrumbs. Stir in the water and bind to make a firm but pliable dough.

Roll out the pastry on a lightly-floured surface and use to line six (11.5-cm/4½-inch) flan tins or dishes. Bake 'blind' in a moderately hot oven (200°C, 400°F, Gas Mark 6) for 15–20 minutes (see page 54). Remove the beans or foil.

Meanwhile prepare the filling: heat the oil in a saucepan. Reserve a few whole mushrooms for the garnish and finely chop the remainder. Add to the oil with the onion and cook until golden, about 10 minutes. Remove from the pan with a slotted spoon and allow to cool.

Cook the whole mushrooms in the pan juices until just cooked. Reserve.

Beat the eggs with the cream, marjoram and seasoning to taste. Divide the mushroom mixture evenly between the pastry cases. Spoon over the cream mixture. Reduce the oven temperature to moderate (180°C, 350°F, Gas Mark 4) and cook the flans for 20 minutes until golden brown and just set. Serve hot, garnished with the reserved cooked whole mushrooms.

Bacon and Spinach Tart

Serves 4

25g (1 oz) butter
350g (12 oz) back bacon, rinds
  removed and chopped
1 onion, peeled and sliced
100g (4 oz) frozen chopped
  spinach, thawed

freshly ground black pepper
1 quantity Shortcrust Pastry
  (see page 12)

Melt the butter in a saucepan. Add the bacon and onion and cook until golden. Add the spinach and pepper to taste, mixing well. Allow to cool.

Meanwhile, roll out the prepared pastry on a lightly-floured surface to a round large enough to line a 20-cm (8-inch) flan tin or dish (see page 54).

Place the spinach filling in the flan and cook in a preheated moderately hot oven (190°C, 375°F, Gas Mark 5) for 30–35 minutes until the pastry is crisp and golden. Serve cut into wedges.

Smoked Haddock and Macaroni Flan

Serves 4-6

*1 quantity Cream Cheese
  Pastry (see page 16)
1 (425-g/15-oz) can macaroni
  cheese
350g (12 oz) cooked smoked
  haddock, flaked*

*50g (2 oz) Cheddar cheese,
  grated
tomato slices and parsley
  sprigs to garnish*

Roll out the prepared pastry on a lightly-floured surface and use
to line a 20-cm (8-inch) flan tin (see page 54). Prick the base well
with a fork and bake 'blind' in a preheated moderately hot oven
(200°C, 400°F, Gas Mark 6) for 15 minutes (see page 54). Remove
the foil or beans.

Place half of the macaroni cheese in the base of the part-cooked
pastry case. Top with the flaked haddock and then the
remaining macaroni cheese. Sprinkle with the grated cheese.
Reduce the oven temperature to moderate (180°C, 350°F, Gas
Mark 4) and cook the flan for a further 15 minutes. Serve warm,
garnished with tomato slices and parsley sprigs.

Kidney and Sage Flan

Serves 4

*3 pig's kidneys, skinned, cored
  and chopped
1 leek, chopped
1 onion, peeled and chopped
25g (1 oz) butter
½ teaspoon dried sage
1 tablespoon chopped fresh
  parsley*

*salt and freshly ground black
  pepper
1 (170-g/6-oz) can evaporated
  milk
2 eggs, beaten
1 quantity Shortcrust Pastry
  (see page 12)*

Mix the kidney with the leek and onion. Melt the butter in a
frying pan. Add the kidney mixture and cook over a gentle heat
until the leek is soft. Add the sage, parsley and seasoning to
taste. Whisk the evaporated milk with the eggs and season
lightly.

Roll out the prepared pastry on a lightly-floured surface and
use to line a 20-cm (8-inch) flan tin or dish (see page 54). Place the
kidney mixture in the pastry case and pour over the milk
mixture. Cook in a preheated moderately hot oven (190°C,
375°F, Gas Mark 5) for 30-35 minutes until golden brown and
set. This flan is delicious served with a mushroom and tomato
salad. Cut into wedges to serve.

Spring Vegetable Quiche

Serves 4-6

1 ¼ quantities Shortcrust
  Pastry (see page 12)
2 carrots, peeled and sliced
2 courgettes, sliced
75g (3 oz) broad beans
50g (2 oz) butter
1 large onion, peeled and
  sliced
50g (2 oz) mushrooms, sliced

1 green pepper, seeds removed
  and sliced
50g (2 oz) Cheddar cheese,
  grated
2 teaspoons dry mustard
  powder
2 eggs
150ml (¼ pint) single cream
salt and freshly ground black
  pepper

Roll out the prepared pastry on a lightly-floured surface and use to line a 25-cm (10-inch) flan tin (see page 54). Prick the base well with a fork and bake 'blind' in a preheated moderately hot oven (200°C, 400°F, Gas Mark 6) for 15 minutes (see page 00). Remove the foil or beans and cook for a further 10-15 minutes. Allow to cool.

Cook the carrots, courgettes and broad beans in boiling salted water for 7 minutes. Drain well. Melt the butter in a pan. Add the onion and sauté until soft. Add the mushrooms and green pepper and cook for 2-3 minutes. Mix the carrots, courgettes and broad beans with the onion, mushrooms and green pepper and place in the pastry case. Sprinkle with the cheese. Add the mustard to the eggs and beat with the single cream and seasoning to taste. Pour over the vegetables.

Reduce the oven temperature to moderate (180°C, 350°F, Gas Mark 4) and cook the flan for 30-35 minutes until golden and set. Serve hot or cold, cut into wedges.

Niçoise Tartlets

Makes 8

1½ quantities Shortcrust
  Pastry (see page 12)
1 (376-g/13¼-oz can tomato
  and onion cook-in-sauce
1 (227-g/8-oz) packet frozen
  green beans, cooked and
  chopped
16 black olives, halved and
  stoned

2 eggs, beaten
1 (56-g/2-oz) can anchovy
  fillets, drained and halved
  lengthways, to garnish
8 black olives, halved and
  stoned, to garnish

Roll out the prepared pastry on a lightly-floured surface and cut out eight rounds large enough to line eight (10-cm/4-inch) tartlet tins. Fit the rounds into the tins (see page 58).

Mix the tomato and onion cook-in-sauce with the green beans, olives and eggs and spoon evenly into the pastry cases. Cook in a preheated moderately hot oven (200°C, 400°F, Gas Mark 6) for 20–25 minutes until the filling has set. Garnish each with two anchovy fillet strips and two olive halves. Serve warm or cold.

Pissaladière

Serves 4

PASTRY
225g (8 oz) wholewheat strong
  plain flour
pinch of salt
50g (2 oz) lard
50g (2 oz) butter
4 tablespoons water
FILLING
2 teaspoons made French
  mustard
25g (1 oz) butter
450g (1 lb) onions, peeled and
  sliced

350g (12 oz) tomatoes, skinned
  and sliced
½ teaspoon chopped fresh
  thyme
1 teaspoon chopped fresh
  chives
½ teaspoon chopped fresh
  basil
75g (3 oz) Gruyère cheese,
  sliced
1 (56-g/2-oz) can anchovy
  fillets, drained
8 black olives

Prepare the pastry: sift the flour and salt into a mixing bowl. Cut the lard and butter into small pieces and rub into the flour until the mixture resembles fine breadcrumbs. Add the water and mix to a soft dough.

Turn onto a lightly-floured surface and knead gently until smooth and free from cracks. Roll out and use to line a 28-cm (11-

120

inch) oval ceramic flan dish or a 23-cm (9-inch) round flan dish set on a baking tray (see page 54). Bake 'blind' in a preheated moderately hot oven (200°C, 400°F, Gas Mark 6) for 15 minutes (see page 54). Remove the beans or foil.

Prepare the filling: spread the mustard on the base of the pastry case. Melt the butter in a shallow pan. Add the onions and sauté until soft but not brown. Drain and place in the pastry case. Cover with a layer of tomatoes and sprinkle with the herbs. Top with the sliced cheese and arrange a lattice of anchovies over the top. Place an olive in each lattice square. Return the flan to the oven and cook for a further 25–30 minutes. Serve hot or cold.

Sausage Pizza Flan

Serves 6

25g (1 oz) butter
1 onion, peeled and finely
    chopped
¼ teaspoon mixed dried herbs
50g (2 oz) plain flour
1 (225-g/8-oz) can peeled
    tomatoes
1 tablespoon tomato purée

150ml (¼ pint) milk
salt and freshly ground black
    pepper
1 quantity Scone Pastry (see
    page 44)
4 large sausages, cooked and
    sliced
parsley sprigs to garnish

Melt the butter in a saucepan. Add the onion and sauté until translucent. Add the herbs and flour and cook for 1 minute. Add the tomatoes with their can juice, tomato purée, milk and seasoning to taste. Bring to the boil, stirring constantly, and cook for 2 minutes. Remove from the heat and allow to cool completely.

Roll out the prepared pastry on a lightly-floured surface to a rectangle 33 × 23cm (13 ×9 inches) and use to line a 28× 18cm (11 × 7 inches) Swiss roll tin. Pour the cooled filling into the pastry case and cook in a preheated moderately hot oven (190°C, 375°F, Gas Mark 5) for 25 minutes until the pastry is golden brown.

Cut the cooked sausages into rings and arrange in two rows down the centre of the flan. Garnish with parsley sprigs before serving.

121

Chicken and Walnut Lemon Quiche

Serves 4

1 quantity Lemon Shortcrust
  Pastry (see page 13)
250g (9 oz) cooked chicken,
  finely chopped
50g (2 oz) walnuts, coarsely
  chopped
100g (4 oz) Gruyère cheese
  grated

¼ teaspoon ground nutmeg
2 eggs, beaten
150ml (¼ pint) milk
salt and freshly ground black
  pepper
watercress sprigs to garnish

Roll out the prepared pastry on a lightly-floured surface and use to line a 20-cm (8-inch) flan tin (see page 54). Prick the base well with a fork and bake 'blind' in a preheated moderately hot oven (200°C, 400°F, Gas Mark 6) for 15 minutes (see page 54). Remove the foil or beans.

Mix the chicken with the walnuts, cheese and nutmeg. Spoon into the pastry case. Mix the eggs with the milk and seasoning to taste and spoon over the chicken filling. Cook the quiche for a further 35 minutes until set and golden brown. Serve warm or cold, cut into wedges and garnished with watercress sprigs.

Asparagus Pinwheel Flan

Serves 4–5

1 quantity Bacon Pastry (see
  page 20)
50g (2 oz) butter
1 onion, peeled and finely
  chopped
25g (1 oz) cooked ham, finely
  chopped
100g (4 oz) mushrooms, finely
  chopped
salt and freshly ground black
  pepper

2½ tablespoons flour
250ml (8 fl oz) hot milk
freshly ground nutmeg
1 large (size 1, 2) egg yolk
2 tablespoons double cream
1 (340-g/12-oz) can asparagus
  spears, drained
2 tablespoons grated
  Parmesan cheese

Roll out the prepared pastry on a lightly-floured surface and use to line a 23-cm (9-inch) flan tin (see page 54). Bake 'blind' in a preheated moderately hot oven (190°C, 375°F, Gas Mark 5) for 15 minutes (see page 54). Remove the foil or beans and cook for a further 10 minutes.

Meanwhile, melt half of the butter in a saucepan. Add the onion and cook for 5 minutes, then add the ham and mushrooms. Cook for a further 5 minutes. Season to taste and set aside. Melt the remaining butter in a pan. Add the flour and cook for 2 minutes. Add the milk gradually and bring to the boil, stirring constantly to make a thick smooth sauce. Season to taste with salt, pepper and nutmeg. Blend the egg yolk with the cream and stir into the sauce.

Place the ham mixture in the pastry case and top with a little of the sauce. Arrange the asparagus spears on top of the sauce like the spokes of a wheel, stalk ends radiating from the centre. Top carefully with the remaining sauce. Sprinkle with the Parmesan cheese and cook the flan for a further 12–15 minutes until the flan has set and turned a rich golden brown. Serve warm.

FAMILY AND FESTIVE MAIN MEALS

Tuna and Chive Plait

Serves 6

2 (198-g/7-oz) cans tuna,
   drained
3 sticks celery, thinly sliced
1 small red pepper, seeds
   removed and chopped
2 tablespoons mayonnaise

1 egg, beaten
2 teaspoons lemon pepper
2 tablespoons snipped chives
½ quantity Puff Pastry (see
   page 25)
poppy seeds to sprinkle

Flake the tuna into a bowl. Add the celery, red pepper, mayonnaise, half the beaten egg, lemon pepper and chives, mixing well to blend.

Roll out the prepared pastry on a lightly-floured surface to a rectangle measuring 30 × 35cm (12 × 14 inches). Place on a dampened baking tray and spread the filling lengthwise down the centre of the pastryn to within 2.5cm (1 inch) of the shorter edges. Brush all the sides with the reserved beaten egg and cut the two long sides into 2-cm (¾-inch) diagonal strips (either side of filling). Fold the end flaps of pastry over the filling then lift the side strips of pastry over the filling to form a plaited effect and press lightly to seal. Brush with beaten egg to glaze and sprinkle with poppy seeds.

Cook in a preheated hot oven (220°C, 425°F, Gas Mark 7) for 35-40 minutes until well risen, golden brown and cooked through. Cover the top with a little foil to prevent over-browning if necessary. Serve hot or cold.

Pork and Pâté Parcels

Serves 6

6 pork loin chops
½ quantity Puff Pastry (see
   page 25)
100g (4 oz) pork liver pâté

salt and freshly ground black
   pepper
beaten egg to glaze

Trim the chops of any excess fat and cook under a preheated moderate grill for 5 minutes each side. Allow to cool.

Roll out the prepared pastry on a lightly-floured surface and cut into six (15-cm/6-inch) squares. Spread both sides of the chops with liver pâté and season well. Wrap each chop in a pastry square, leaving the bone protruding and sealing well.

Place on a dampened baking tray and brush with beaten egg to glaze. Cook in a preheated moderately hot oven (190°C, 375°F, Gas Mark 5) for 30 minutes. Serve hot or cold.

Beef, Chestnut and Bacon Parcels

Serves 4

225g (8 oz) rump steak, cubed
75g (3 oz) streaky bacon, rinds
  removed and chopped
50g (2 oz) pâté de foie
1 tablespoon unsweetened
  chestnut purée
6 spring onions, trimmed and
  chopped

½ bunch watercress, trimmed
  and chopped
salt and freshly ground black
  pepper
½ quantity Puff Pastry (see
  page 25)
beaten egg to glaze

Mix the steak with the bacon, pâté, chestnut purée, spring onions, watercress and seasoning to taste.

Roll out the prepared pastry on a lightly-floured surface to a 25-cm (10-inch) square then cut into sixteen equal squares. Brush the edges of the pastry with beaten egg. Divide the filling into eight portions and place on eight of the pastry squares. Cover with the remaining pastry squares. Trim, seal and flute the edges.

Place on a dampened baking tray and brush with beaten egg to glaze. Cook in a preheated hot oven (230°C, 450°F, Gas Mark 8) for 25 minutes, reduce the oven temperature to moderate (180°C, 350°F, Gas Mark 4) and cook for a further 15 minutes. Serve hot with vegetables or salad in season.

Lamb Parcel

Serves 6

1 (675-g/1½-lb) boned fillet
  end of lamb
25g (1 oz) butter
1 small onion, peeled and
  chopped
100g (4 oz) button mushrooms

150ml (½ pint) soured cream
2 teaspoons paprika pepper
½ quantity Puff Pastry (see
  page 25)
beaten egg to glaze

Cut the lamb into thick slices. Melt the butter in a frying pan. Add the lamb and brown on all sides. Remove with a slotted spoon and allow to cool. Add the onion to the pan juices and cook for 5 minutes. Add the mushrooms and cook for a further 2–3 minutes. Stir in the soured cream and paprika. Leave until cold.

Roll out the prepared pastry on a lightly-floured surface to about 3mm (⅛ inch) thick and to a rectangle measuring 30 × 20cm (12 × 8 inches). Place half the lamb slices in the centre of the pastry. Top with the mushroom mixture and the remaining lamb slices. Brush the edges of the pastry with beaten egg and fold over to completely enclose the filling, sealing well (see page 87).

Place on a dampened baking tray and brush with beaten egg to glaze. Use any pastry trimmings to decorate the parcel as liked. Brush again with beaten egg to glaze. Cook in a preheated hot oven (220°C, 425°F, Gas Mark 7) for 30 minutes. Reduce the oven temperature to moderate (160°C, 325°F, Gas Mark 3) and cook for a further 50-60 minutes. Cover the top with a little foil to prevent over-browning if necessary. Cut into slices to serve.

Duck and Apricot Picnic Slice

Serves 8-10

175g (6 oz) fresh white breadcrumbs
50g (2 oz) dried apricots, coarsely chopped
50g (2 oz) walnuts, chopped
25g (1 oz) fresh parsley, coarsely chopped
grated rind and juice of 1 large orange
1 dessert apple, peeled, cored and chopped
1 egg, beaten
1 (2.25-kg/5-lb) duck, boned
salt and freshly ground black pepper
½ quantity Puff Pastry (see page 25)
beaten egg to glaze

Mix the breadcrumbs with the apricots, walnuts, parsley, orange rind, orange juice, apple and beaten egg. Lay the duck, skinside downwards on a board. Top with the stuffing mixture, fold over the ends and sides to form a long, neat sausage shape and secure with string. Rub generously with salt and freshly ground black pepper. Place on a trivet in a roasting tin. Cook in a preheated moderate oven (180°C, 350°F, Gas Mark 4) for 1½ hours and allow to cool completely. Remove the string.

Roll out the prepared pastry on a lightly-floured surface to a rectangle large enough to completely enclose the duck. Place the duck on the pastry, brush the edges with beaten egg and fold over to completely enclose, sealing well. Brush with beaten egg to glaze and decorate with the pastry trimmings as liked. Brush again with beaten egg. Increase the oven temperature to moderately hot (200°C, 400°F, Gas Mark 6) and cook the slice for 40-45 minutes. Cover the top with a little foil to prevent over-browning if necessary. Serve cold, cut into slices with mixed salad.

Tuna, Oyster and Spinach Vol-au-vent

Serves 6

½ quantity Puff Pastry (see page 25)
beaten egg to glaze
1 (300-g/10.6-oz) packet frozen cut leaf spinach
1 (198-g/7-oz) can tuna in brine
1 (105-g/3⅔-oz) can smoked oysters, drained
25g (1 oz) butter
1 small onion, peeled and finely chopped

25g (1 oz) flour
150ml (¼ pint) milk
¼ teaspoon ground cloves
salt and freshly ground black pepper
1 tablespoon medium sherry
3 tablespoons single cream
2 teaspoons chopped fresh parsley

Roll out the prepared pastry on a lightly-floured surface and cut out two (20-cm/8-inch) rounds. Place one round on a dampened baking tray. Cut out a circle measuring 14cm (5½ inches) from the middle of the second round and reserve. Dampen the outer edge of the ring of pastry with water and neatly press around the edge of the first round of pastry to form a vol-au-vent (see page 61). Prick the centre of the pastry with a fork and mark a triangular pattern, using a sharp knife, over the outer edge of the vol-au-vent. Place the reserved lid on a dampened baking tray and mark in a triangular pattern as before. Brush the lid and the outer edges of the vol-au-vent with beaten egg to glaze, taking care not to get any around the edges of the pastry as this will prevent it from rising. Cook in a preheated hot oven (220°C, 425°F, Gas Mark 7) for 15–20 minutes until well risen. Reduce the oven temperature to moderate (180°C, 350°F, Gas Mark 4) and cook for a further 5–10 minutes until golden brown. Keep warm.

Meanwhile, cook the spinach according to packet instructions and drain well. Drain and flake the tuna, reserving any can juices. Mix the tuna with the spinach and oysters.

Melt the butter in a small saucepan. Add the onion and cook for 6–8 minutes or until soft. Stir in the flour and cook for 1 minute. Gradually add the milk, ground cloves and tuna can juices. Bring to the boil, stirring constantly, then simmer for 3–5 minutes. Fold in the tuna mixture, seasoning to taste and sherry. Cook for a further 2–3 minutes, stir in the cream and parsley and mix well.

Spoon the mixture into the warm vol-au-vent case and serve hot, with a salad garnish if liked.

Sole, Caper and Egg Envelopes

Serves 4

1 quantity Rough Puff Pastry
  (see page 28)
450g (1 lb) sole fillets, skinned
  and cut into four equal pieces
2 hard-boiled eggs, sliced
1 (213-g/7½-oz) can creamed
  mushrooms
	1 teaspoon lemon juice
	4 teaspoons chopped capers
	1 tablespoon snipped chives
	salt and freshly ground black
	  pepper
	beaten egg to glaze

Roll out the prepared pastry on a lightly-floured surface and cut into four (13-cm/5-inch) squares. Place on dampened baking trays.

Place a piece of the fish on each pastry square and top with the egg. Mix the creamed mushrooms with the lemon juice, capers, chives and seasoning to taste. Spoon over the egg. Brush the edges of the pastry squares with beaten egg. Bring the corners of each square together and seal the edges to form envelope shapes (see page 62). Make a small hole in the top of each envelope to aid the escape of steam. Brush with beaten egg to glaze and decorate with any pastry trimmings as liked.

Cook in a preheated hot oven (220°C, 425°F, Gas Mark 7) for 20–25 minutes until well-risen, golden brown and cooked through.

Serve hot with salad or stuffed baked tomatoes.

Cheese and Sage Pork Roll with Soured Cream

Serves 2

1 (350-g/12-oz) pork tenderloin
¼ teaspoon ground nutmeg
salt and freshly ground black
  pepper
4 tablespoons chopped fresh
  sage
100g (4 oz) Gruyère cheese,
  thinly sliced

25g (1 oz) butter
½ quantity Rough Puff Pastry
  (see page 28)
beaten egg to glaze
1 tablespoon grated Parmesan
  cheese
150ml (¼ pint) soured cream

Beat the pork between two sheets of dampened greaseproof paper until very thin. Sprinkle with the nutmeg and seasoning to taste. Completely cover with the sage and cheese then roll up and secure with string. Place in a roasting tin and cook in a preheated moderate oven (160°C, 325°F, Gas Mark 3) for 1 hour. Remove and allow to cool slightly.

Roll out the prepared pastry on a lightly-floured surface to a rectangle large enough to completely enclose the pork roll. Place the pork on the pastry, brush the pastry edges with beaten egg and secure well. Place, seam-side down, on a dampened baking tray. Brush with beaten egg to glaze and decorate with any pastry trimmings as liked. Sprinkle with the Parmesan cheese. Increase the oven temperature to hot (220°C, 425°F, Gas Mark 7) and cook the roll for 25–30 minutes until well-risen and golden. Serve hot, cut into slices with the soured cream.

Seafood Coulibiac

Serves 4

1 tablespoon oil
1 onion, peeled and chopped
50g (2 oz) bacon, rinds
  removed and chopped
50g (2 oz) mushrooms, sliced
225g (8 oz) cooked haddock or
  cod, skinned and flaked
100g (4 oz) peeled prawns
1 (105-g/3⅔-oz) can smoked
  oysters, drained

1 tablespoon chopped fresh
  parsley
salt and freshly ground black
  pepper
grated rind of 1 lemon
150ml (¼ pint) double cream,
  lightly whipped
1 quantity Rough Puff or Flaky
  Pastry (see page 28 or 32)
beaten egg to glaze

Heat the oil in a pan. Add the onion and bacon and cook until lightly browned, about 5–8 minutes. Add the mushrooms, mix well and allow to cool.

Add the fish, prawns, oysters, parsley, seasoning to taste, lemon rind and double cream. Mix well to blend.

Roll out the prepared pastry on a lightly-floured surface to a 35-cm (14-inch) square. Place on a dampened baking tray. Place the fish mixture in the centre of the square. Brush the edges with beaten egg and bring the pastry corners to the centre to meet and form an envelope shape (see page 62). Seal and crimp the edges well. Brush with beaten egg to glaze and decorate with any pastry trimmings, cut into small fish shapes.

Cook in a preheated hot oven (220°C, 425°F, Gas Mark 7) for 25–30 minutes until well-risen, golden brown and cooked through.

Pork and Pimiento Slice

Serves 6

450g (1 lb) large pork sausages,
  cut into bite-sized pieces
2 canned pimientos, finely
  chopped
1 small onion, peeled and
  finely chopped
75g (3 oz) streaky bacon, rinds
  removed and chopped

1 egg, beaten
salt and freshly ground black
  pepper
1 quantity Shortcrust Pastry
  (see page 12)

Mix the sausages with the pimiento, onion and bacon. Add almost all of the egg and seasoning to taste.

Roll out three-quarters of the prepared pastry on a lightly-floured surface to a rectangle measuring 30 × 25cm (12 × 10 inches). Spread the sausage mixture lengthwise down the centre of the pastry. Brush the edges with beaten egg then fold over and seal to make a giant sausage roll. Place on a greased baking tray, seam-side down. Roll out the remaining pastry and cut into 2-cm (¾-inch) strips. Brush the pastry roll with beaten egg to glaze and arrange the pastry strips on top of the roll in a trellis pattern. Seal carefully and trim if necessary. Brush again with beaten egg.

Cook in a preheated moderately hot oven (190°C, 375°F, Gas Mark 5) for about 40 minutes until golden brown and cooked through. Serve hot or cold, cut into thick slices.

Slipper Pudding

Serves 4

1 quantity Suet Crust Pastry
(see page 38)
1 (675-g/1½-lb) piece slipper
bacon, soaked overnight in
cold water

25g (1 oz) flour
100g (4 oz) button mushrooms,
quartered
freshly ground black pepper
juice of ½ lemon

Roll out the prepared pastry on a lightly-floured surface to a round about 5cm (2 inches) larger than the diameter of a 900-ml (1½-pint) pudding basin. Cut a quarter section from the pastry round and reserve for a lid (see page 67).

Lift the remaining piece of pastry and ease it into the basin, pinching the two cut edges together to seal and moulding the pastry onto the base and around the sides of the basin (see page 67).

Trim the bacon and cut into small bite-sized cubes. Add the flour and toss well to coat. Fill the pastry-lined basin with alternate layers of bacon and mushrooms, seasoning between each layer with pepper. Pour over the lemon juice.

Roll out the remaining pastry to a round large enough to make a lid. Dampen the pastry edges with water and cover with the lid. Pinch the edges together firmly to seal. Cover either with a piece of greaseproof paper, pleated in the centre and foil or with greaseproof paper and a pudding cloth. Secure with string. Steam the pudding over a gentle heat for 3–4 hours until cooked and well risen, checking the water level regularly. Serve hot with fresh vegetables in season.

Ham and Pepper Roly-Poly

Serves 4

25g (1 oz) butter or margarine
1 clove garlic, peeled and
crushed
1 onion, peeled and chopped
1 small green pepper, seeds
removed and chopped
1 small red pepper, seeds
removed and chopped

175g (6 oz) lean cooked ham,
coarsely chopped
¼ teaspoon dried oregano
salt and freshly ground black
pepper
1 quantity Suet Crust Pastry
(see page 38)

Melt the butter or margarine in a pan. Add the garlic, onion and peppers and cook over a low heat until just soft, about 6–8 minutes. Stir in the ham and oregano. Drain away any excess liquid and season to taste.

Roll out the prepared pastry on a lightly-floured surface to a rectangle 25 × 30cm (10 × 12 inches). Spread the ham filling evenly over the pastry to within 2cm (¾ inch) of the edges. Dampen the pastry edges with water, then turn in the edges on two long sides and one short side and brush them again with water. Roll up, from the short folded edge like a Swiss roll. Wrap loosely in greased foil and place on a baking tray. Twist the ends of the foil to seal.

Cook in a preheated moderately hot oven (190°C, 375°F, Gas Mark 5) for 40 minutes. Serve with a hot tomato sauce if liked and vegetables in season.

Tarragon and Thyme Turkey Parcel

Serves 4

½ quantity Puff Pastry (see page 25)
40g (1½ oz) butter
40g (1½ oz) flour
175ml (6 fl oz) milk
1 tablespoon tarragon and thyme mustard

225g (8 oz) cooked turkey meat, chopped
1 (225-g/8-oz) packet frozen mixed vegetables
salt and freshly ground black pepper
milk to glaze

Roll out the prepared pastry on a lightly-floured surface to a rectangle measuring 35 × 30cm (14 × 12 inches), reserving any pastry trimmings.

Melt the butter in a saucepan. Add the flour and cook for 1 minute. Gradually add the milk and cook until smooth and thickened, stirring. Stir in the mustard, turkey, vegetables and seasoning to taste. Allow to cool.

Spread the turkey mixture down the centre of the pastry. Dampen the pastry edges with water, fold over and seal firmly. Roll out the pastry trimmings to form a 'string' to knot around the pastry parcel. Place the parcel, seam-side down, on a dampened baking tray. Tuck the pastry string around and under the parcel.

Brush with milk to glaze and cook in a preheated hot oven (220°C, 425°F, Gas Mark 7) for 25–30 minutes. Serve hot or cold, cut into thick slices.

Friday Foldovers

Serves 4

POTATO PASTRY
900g (2 lb) potatoes, peeled,
  boiled and puréed
100g (4 oz) plain flour
100g (4 oz) butter
salt and freshly ground black
  pepper

FILLING
8 cooked sausages
8 tablespoons herby mustard
beaten egg to glaze

Prepare the pastry: mix the potato purée with the flour and butter to make a smooth dough. Season well with salt and freshly ground black pepper. Divide into eight equal pieces.

Roll out each piece on a lightly-floured surface to a 13-cm (5-inch) square, or pat out on a lightly-floured surface. Place a sausage in the centre of each square and top with 1 tablespoon mustard. Fold the pastry over to completely enclose the sausage and crimp the edges together to seal.

Place on a greased baking tray and brush with beaten egg to glaze. Cook in a preheated moderately hot oven (200°C, 400°F, Gas Mark 6) for 30 minutes until golden brown. Serve hot with a tomato sauce.

Mustard Beef Hot Pot with Herby Choux Topping

Serves 4-6

900g (2 lb) lean braising beef,
  cut into bite-sized cubes
1 tablespoon seasoned flour
50g (2 oz) butter
1 tablespoon oil
4 rashers back bacon, rinds
  removed and chopped
2 large onions, peeled and
  sliced
2 cloves garlic,
  peeled and crushed

300ml (½ pint) beef stock
300ml (½ pint) brown ale
2 tablespoons made French
  mustard
2 bay leaves
salt and freshly ground black
  pepper
1 quantity Herby Choux
  Pastry (see page 36)

Toss the beef in the flour to coat. Heat the butter and oil in a pan. Add the bacon and sauté until lightly browned. Remove with a slotted spoon and place in a medium-sized casserole. Add the onion to the pan juices and cook for 5 minutes. Remove with a slotted spoon and place in the casserole. Add the meat to the pan and cook until lightly-browned on all sides, adding the garlic for the last few minutes cooking time. Remove with a slotted spoon and place in the casserole.

Add the stock and ale to the pan juices. Stir in the mustard and then pour over the casserole ingredients. Add the bay leaves and seasoning to taste. Cover and cook in a preheated moderate oven (160°C, 325°F, Gas Mark 3) for 2 hours.

Meanwhile, spoon the prepared pastry into a piping bag fitted with a large plain nozzle. Pipe choux buns around the edge of the casserole.

Increase the oven temperature to hot (220°C, 425°F, Gas Mark 7) and cook, uncovered, for 20 minutes. Reduce the oven temperature to moderate (180°C, 350°F, Gas Mark 4) and cook for a further 20 minutes.

Kentish Chicken Pudding

Serves 4-6

1 quantity Suet Crust Pastry (see page 38)
225g (8 oz) salted belly pork, chopped
450g (1 lb) raw chicken meat, chopped

salt and freshly ground black pepper
2 onions, peeled and chopped
2 teaspoons chopped fresh parsley
150ml (¼ pint) chicken stock

Roll out the prepared pastry on a lightly-floured surface to a round about 5cm (2 inches) larger than the diameter of a 1-litre (2-pint) pudding basin. Cut a quarter section from the pastry round and reserve for a lid (see page 67).

Lift the remaining piece of pastry and ease it into the basin, pinching the two cut edges together to seal and moulding the pastry onto the base and around the sides of the basin (see page 67).

Mix the pork with the chicken and seasoning to taste in a bowl. Add the onion and parsley and toss well to mix. Place in the pastry-lined basin and cover with the stock.

Roll out the remaining pastry to a round large enough to make a lid. Dampen the pastry edges with water and cover with the lid. Pinch the edges together firmly to seal. Cover with a piece of pleated foil and secure with string. Steam the pudding over a gentle heat for 2½-3 hours, checking the water level regularly. Serve hot with cooked mushrooms and vegetables in season.

Casseroled Pork in Wine with Dumplings

Serves 4-6

1.8kg (4 lb) pork shoulder, boned and cut into bite-sized pieces
4 tablespoons seasoned flour
finely grated rind of ½ lemon
3 tablespoons oil
25g (1 oz) butter
3 large onions, peeled and chopped
2 cloves garlic, peeled and finely chopped
675g (1½ lb) carrots, peeled and thickly sliced

225g (8 oz) back bacon, rinds removed and chopped
1 bouquet garni
piece of orange rind
1 teaspoon dried herbes de Provence
150ml (¼ pint) dry red wine
450ml (¾ pint) beef stock
½ quantity Suet Crust Pastry (see page 38)
finely chopped fresh herbs to garnish

Toss the pork in the flour with the lemon rind. Heat the oil and butter in a large flameproof casserole. Add half of the meat and cook over a high heat until browned on all sides. Remove with a slotted spoon and reserve. Add the remaining meat and cook in the same way. Remove with a slotted spoon and add the onion and garlic. Cook over a low heat for 5 minutes. Add the carrots and bacon and cook for a further 5 minutes. Return the meat to the casserole with the bouquet garni, piece of orange rind herbes de Provence, wine and stock. Cover and cook in a preheated moderate oven (160°C, 325°F, Gas Mark 3) for about 2 hours.

Meanwhile, divide the prepared pastry into eight equal pieces. Roll each piece into a ball about the same size as a walnut.

Place the casserole over a moderate heat on top of the cooker and place the dumplings on top of the casserole. Cover and cook for about 25 minutes until the dumplings are well-risen and fluffy. Serve the casserole and dumplings sprinkled with freshly chopped herbs.

Brunch-time Mille Feuilles

Serves 4-6

½ quantity Puff Pastry (see page 25)
25g (1 oz) butter
100g (4 oz) back bacon, rinds removed and chopped
6 eggs

2 tablespoons double cream
salt and freshly ground black pepper
1 tablespoon snipped chives
sliced tomato and watercress sprigs to garnish

Roll out the prepared pastry on a lightly-floured surface to make three rectangles measuring 30 × 15cm (12 × 6 inches). Place on dampened baking trays and prick well with a fork (see page 69). Using a sharp knife, mark one rectangle with a diamond pattern. Cook in a preheated hot oven (220°C, 425°F, Gas Mark 7) for 12-15 minutes until well-risen, golden brown and crisp.

Meanwhile, melt the butter in a saucepan. Add the bacon and cook until crisp. Beat the eggs with the cream, seasoning to taste and chives. Stir into the bacon and cook, over a gentle heat, until lightly scrambled.

Spread half of the mixture on the top of an unmarked pastry rectangle. Cover with the second unmarked rectangle. Top with the remaining egg and bacon mixture. Finally cover with the diamond-patterned rectangle. Garnish with tomato slices and watercress sprigs. Serve warm, cut into thick slices.

Steak and Kidney Pudding

Serves 4

1 quantity Light Suet Crust Pastry (see page 38)	25g (1 oz) seasoned flour
	1 teaspoon mixed dried herbs
675g (1½ lb) lean stewing beef, cubed	150ml (¼ pint) beef stock
225g (8 oz) ox kidney, cored and cubed	1 tablespoon Worcestershire sauce
1 onion, peeled and finely chopped	

Roll out the prepared pastry on a lightly-floured surface to a round about 5cm (2 inches) larger than the diameter of a 1-litre (2-pint) pudding basin. Cut a quarter section from the pastry round and reserve for a lid (see page 67).

Lift the remaining piece of pastry and ease it into the basin, pinching the two cut edges together to seal and moulding the pastry onto the base and around the sides of the basin (see page 67).

Toss the beef, kidney and onion in the seasoned flour and place in the pastry-lined basin. Sprinkle the herbs over the meat. Add the stock and Worcestershire sauce.

Roll out the remaining pastry to a round large enough to make a lid. Dampen the pastry edges with water and cover with the lid. Pinch the edges together firmly to seal. Cover with a piece of pleated foil and secure with string. Steam the pudding over a gentle heat for 4 hours, checking the water level regularly. Serve hot with vegetables in season.

Buffet Turkey and Pepper Slice

Serves 8

½ quantity Rough Puff Pastry
  (see page 28)
100g (4 oz) butter
150ml (¼ pint) water
100g (3½ oz) plain flour
2 eggs, beaten
1 onion, peeled and sliced
100g (4 oz) streaky bacon,
  rinds removed and chopped
1 large red pepper, seeds
  removed and sliced
1 tablespoon dry mustard
  powder

300ml (½ pint) milk
2 teaspoons lemon juice
150ml (¼ pint) single cream
400g (14 oz) cooked turkey,
  skinned and cut into bite-
  sized pieces
2 tablespoons snipped chives
salt and freshly ground black
  pepper
75g (3 oz) thinly sliced garlic
  sausage
stuffed olives to garnish

Roll out the prepared pastry on a lightly-floured surface to a rectangle measuring 35 × 20cm (14 × 8 inches). Prick well with a fork and place on a dampened baking tray.

Place 50g (2 oz) of the butter in a saucepan with the water and bring to the boil. Quickly add 65g (2½ oz) of the flour, mixing well. Allow to cool slightly then beat in the eggs, keeping the mixture smooth and thick. Place in a piping bag fitted with a large star-shaped nozzle and pipe swirls down each long side of the pastry rectangle. Cook in a preheated moderately hot oven (200°C, 400°F, Gas Mark 6) for 25–30 minutes until well-risen and golden brown.

Meanwhile, melt the remaining butter in a pan. Add the onion, bacon and red pepper and cook for 8–10 minutes until cooked and lightly brown. Stir in the remaining flour and mustard and cook for 1 minute. Gradually add the milk, mixing to make a smooth sauce. Cook for 2–3 minutes, stirring constantly. Add the lemon juice and allow to cool.

When cool, stir in the single cream, turkey, chives and seasoning to taste. Reheat but do not allow to boil. Spoon into the warm pastry case and garnish with thinly sliced garlic sausage, rolled into cornets and filled with a stuffed olive. Slice to serve.

Filet de Boeuf en Croûte

Serves 6

*900g (2 lb) fillet of beef, about
   20–23cm (8–9 inches) long
salt and freshly ground black
   pepper
50g (2 oz) butter
1 tablespoon oil*

*225g (8 oz) pâté de foie
½ quantity Puff Pastry (see
   page 25)
beaten egg to glaze
watercress sprigs to garnish*

Place the meat on a board and, using a sharp knife, trim away any excess fat. Sprinkle liberally with salt and freshly ground black pepper. Tie some fine string around the meat at intervals to form it into a neat shape. Continue the string around the ends and across to the other side as for a parcel and tie firmly.

Heat half the butter with the oil in a frying pan. Add the meat and fry until well browned on all sides, turning frequently. Place in a roasting tin and dot with the remaining butter. Cook in the top of a preheated moderately hot oven (200°C, 400°F, Gas Mark 6) for 10 minutes. Remove, leave until cold and then remove the string.

Season the pâté to taste and beat until smooth. Using a small palette knife, spread the pâté over the top and sides of the meat.

Roll out the prepared pastry on a lightly-floured surface to about 3mm (⅛ inch) thick and to a rectangle large enough to completely enclose the meat. Place the meat, pâté side down on the centre of the pastry. Spread pâté over the rest of the meat. Brush one long side of the pastry with beaten egg. Fold the unbrushed side over the meat, fold up the second side and press firmly together. Trim the ends of the pastry at an angle, cutting it straight off close to the meat. Reserve the trimmings for decoration. Brush the upper surfaces of the trimmed ends with beaten egg and fold diagonally across the ends of the parcel (see page 76).

Brush the pastry surface with beaten egg to glaze and decorate with the pastry trimmings as liked. Brush again with beaten egg. Cook in a preheated hot oven (220°C, 425°F, Gas Mark 7) for 40 minutes until well-risen, golden and cooked. Serve hot, garnished with watercress sprigs.

Guard of Honour en Croûte with Onion Sauce

Serves 6

*2 best end racks of lamb,
  chined
salt and freshly ground black
  pepper
2 teaspoons dried rosemary
½ quantity Puff or Rough Puff
  Pastry (see page 25 or 28)
beaten egg to glaze
SAUCE
20g (¾ oz) butter*

*2 onions, peeled and chopped
15g (½ oz) flour
300ml (½ pint) milk
½ teaspoon ground nutmeg
1 tablespoon double cream
2 tablespoons dry white wine
sprigs fresh rosemary to
  garnish (optional)*

Trim the lamb free of excess fat and scrape away the meat and fat from the bone ends to about 2.5cm (1 inch) depth. Lock the bone ends together to form a guard of honour shape. Season generously and sprinkle with rosemary. Place in a roasting tin and cook in a preheated moderately hot oven (200°C, 400°F, Gas Mark 6) for 45 minutes. Remove and allow to cool.

Roll out the prepared pastry on a lightly-floured surface to a rectangle large enough to completely enclose the lamb but leaving the bones protruding. Place the lamb on the pastry. Dampen the pastry edges and seal well. Place on a baking sheet. Brush with beaten egg to glaze and decorate with any pastry trimmings as liked. Cook in a preheated hot oven (220°C, 425°F, Gas Mark 7) for 30–40 minutes until well-risen, golden brown and cooked through.

Meanwhile prepare the sauce: melt the butter in a pan. Add the onions and lightly fry for 5–7 minutes. Remove and liquidise until smooth. Return to the pan with the flour and cook for 3–4 minutes. Gradually add the milk, stirring constantly to make a smooth sauce. Add the nutmeg, cream and wine. Taste and adjust the seasoning if necessary.

Serve the lamb hot, cut into chops, with the onion sauce. Garnish with sprigs of rosemary if liked.

Cornish Pasties

Makes 4

225g (8 oz) lean beef steak
2 medium potatoes, peeled and
  diced
1 onion, peeled and chopped
½ teaspoon mixed dried herbs
1 tablespoon chopped fresh
  parsley

salt and freshly ground black
  pepper
2 tablespoons beef stock
1½ quantities Shortcrust
  Pastry (see page 12)
beaten egg to glaze

Shred the meat finely and mix with the potato, onion, dried herbs, parsley and seasoning to taste. Moisten with the beef stock.

Roll out the prepared pastry on a lightly-floured surface and cut out four (20-cm/8-inch) rounds. Divide the meat and vegetable mixture between the rounds. Dampen the pastry edges with water and draw together to make a seam across the top. Crimp the edges decoratively (see page 86).

Place on a greased baking tray and brush with beaten egg to glaze. Cook in a preheated hot oven (220°C, 425°F, Gas Mark 7) for 15 minutes. Reduce the oven temperature to moderate (160°C, 325°F, Gas Mark 3) and cook for a further 50-60 minutes.

SAVOURY PIES

Sausage and Cream Cheese Picnic Pie

Serves 4-6

450g (1 lb) pork sausagemeat
2 teaspoons finely chopped
    fresh mixed herbs or 1
    teaspoon dried
salt and freshly ground black
    pepper

½ quantity Puff Pastry (see
    page 25)
100g (4 oz) cream cheese
1 tablespoon tomato purée
beaten egg to glaze

Mix the sausagemeat with the herbs and seasoning to taste. Divide in half and shape into two (15-cm/6-inch) rounds.

Roll out the prepared pastry on a lightly-floured surface and cut out one 18-cm (7-inch) round and one 20-cm (8-inch) round, reserving any pastry for decoration.

Place the larger round on a dampened baking tray and top with a sausagemeat round. Beat the cream cheese with the tomato purée and spread on top of the sausagemeat. Cover with the remaining sausagemeat round. Brush the pastry edges with beaten egg and top with the remaining pastry round. Seal the edges well and flute or crimp if liked. Decorate with any pastry trimmings as liked.

Brush with beaten egg to glaze and cook in a preheated moderately hot oven (200°C, 400°F, Gas Mark 6) for about 30–40 minutes until well-risen, golden brown and cooked through. Serve hot or cold.

Beef Sausage and Horseradish Pie

Serves 6

1 tablespoon oil
450g (1 lb) beef sausages
4 small leeks, sliced
100g (4 oz) button mushrooms
4 tablespoons double cream
3–4 teaspoons grated
    horseradish

freshly ground black pepper
¼ quantity Puff Pastry (see
    page 25)
beaten egg to glaze

Heat the oil in a pan. Add the sausages and fry until golden and cooked, about 8–10 minutes. Remove with a slotted spoon and cut into bite-sized pieces. Add the leeks and mushrooms to the pan and cook for 3–5 minutes. Strain off excess fat. Add the cream, horseradish, sausages and black pepper to taste. Turn into a medium pie dish and allow to cool slightly.

Roll out the prepared pastry on a lightly-floured surface to a round about 4cm (1½ inches) larger than the pie dish. Trim a 2.5-cm (1-inch) strip from the edge of the pastry and use to line the dampened rim of the dish. Dampen the pastry rim with water and cover with the lid (see page 50). Trim, seal and flute the edges. Use any pastry trimmings to decorate the pie as liked.

Brush with beaten egg to glaze and cook in a preheated hot oven (220°C, 425°F, Gas Mark 7) for 15 minutes. Reduce the oven temperature to moderately hot (200°C, 400°F, Gas Mark 6) and cook for a further 15–20 minutes until well-risen, golden brown and cooked. Serve hot.

Spicy Beef and Walnut Mid-winter Pie

Serves 6-8

25g (1 oz) beef dripping
1.25kg (2½ lb) braising or stewing steak, cut into bite-sized pieces
10 small button onions, peeled
6 carrots, peeled and chopped
1 small turnip, peeled and chopped
4 sticks celery, chopped
100g (4 oz) walnut halves
2 tablespoons flour
1 tablespoon dry mustard powder
salt and freshly ground black pepper
300ml (½ pint) beef stock
2 teaspoons mixed dried herbs
1 teaspoon Worcestershire sauce
¼ quantity Puff Pastry (see page 25)
beaten egg to glaze

Melt the dripping in a large saucepan. Add the beef and cook quickly on all sides to brown. Add the onions and allow to brown. Add the carrot, turnip, celery and walnuts and cook for 6–8 minutes until lightly softened. Mix the flour with the mustard and seasoning to taste and stir into the meat and vegetable mixture. Cook until the flour browns lightly. Gradually add the stock, stirring well. Add the herbs and Worcestershire sauce. Cover and simmer, over a low heat, for 45 minutes. Turn into a medium pie dish and allow to cool slightly.

Roll out the prepared pastry on a lightly-floured surface to a round about 4cm (1½ inches) larger than the pie dish. Trim a 2.5-cm (1-inch) strip from the edge of the pastry and use to line the dampened rim of the dish. Dampen the pastry rim with water and cover with the lid (see page 50). Trim, seal and flute the edges. Use any pastry trimmings to decorate the pie as liked.

Brush with beaten egg to glaze and cook in a preheated hot oven (220°C, 425°F, Gas Mark 7) for 30 minutes. Reduce the oven temperature to moderate (180°C, 350°F, Gas Mark 4) and cook for a further 20 minutes. Cover the top with a little foil to prevent over-browning if necessary. Serve steaming hot.

Individual Kidney and Sausage Pies

Serves 4

25g (1 oz) butter
1 tablespoon oil
20 button onions, peeled
8 lamb's kidneys, cored and
    sliced
225g (8 oz) chipolata sausages,
    cut into bite-sized pieces
1 tablespoon wholemeal flour
300ml (½ pint) beef stock

175ml (6 fl oz) dry red wine
225g (8 oz) small button
    mushrooms
½ teaspoon dried thyme
salt and freshly ground black
    pepper
½ quantity Puff Pastry (see
    page 25)
beaten egg to glaze

Melt the butter and oil in a large saucepan. Add the onions and cook quickly on all sides to brown. Add the kidney and sausages and cook for about 10 minutes until lightly browned. Remove with a slotted spoon. Sprinkle the flour into the pan and cook for 1 minute. Gradually add the stock and wine, stirring well. Return the onion, kidney and sausage mixture to the pan. Add the mushrooms, thyme and seasoning to taste. Cover and simmer for 15–20 minutes. Spoon into four individual pie dishes and allow to cool slightly.

Roll out the prepared pastry on a lightly-floured surface and cut into four rounds about 4cm (1½ inches) larger than the pie dishes. Trim a 2.5-cm (1-inch) strip from each and use to line the dampened rims of each dish. Dampen the pastry rims with water and cover with the lids (see page 50). Trim, seal and flute the edges. Use any pastry trimmings to decorate the pies as liked.

Brush with beaten egg to glaze and cook in a preheated moderately hot oven (200°C, 400°F, Gas Mark 6) for 10 minutes. Reduce the oven temperature to moderate (180°C, 350°F, Gas Mark 4) and cook for a further 15 minutes until the pies are well-risen, golden brown and cooked through. Serve hot.

Steak, Kidney and Mushroom Pie

Serves 4-6

675g (1½ lb) chuck steak, cut
  into bite-sized pieces
1 tablespoon seasoned flour
50g (2 oz) beef dripping
100g (4 oz) lamb's kidneys,
  cored and quartered
2 onions, peeled and sliced

175g (6 oz) mushrooms, sliced
150ml (¼ pint) beef stock
150ml (¼ pint) dry red wine
¼ quantity Puff Pastry (see
  page 25)
beaten egg to glaze

Coat the steak in the seasoned flour. Melt the dripping in a
large saucepan. Add the steak and cook quickly on all sides to
brown. Add the kidney and fry until brown. Remove with a
slotted spoon. Add the onion to the pan juices and cook for 5
minutes. Add the mushrooms and cook for a further 2–3
minutes. Return the meat to the pan, add the stock and wine,
cover and simmer for 1½ hours. Turn into a medium pie dish
and allow to cool slightly.

Roll out the prepared pastry on a lightly-floured surface to a
round about 4cm (1½ inches) larger than the pie dish. Trim a
2.5-cm (1-inch) strip from the edge of the pastry and use to line
the dampened rim of the dish. Dampen the pastry rim with
water and cover with the lid (see page 50). Trim, seal and flute
the edges. Use any pastry trimmings to decorate the pie as
liked.

Brush with beaten egg to glaze and cook in a preheated hot
oven (220°C, 425°F, Gas Mark 7) for 35–45 minutes until well-
risen and golden brown. Serve hot with vegetables in season.

Cheshire Cheese and Tattie Pie

Serves 6-8

½ quantity Puff Pastry (see
  page 25)
350g (12 oz) cooked new
  potatoes, sliced
salt and freshly ground black
  pepper
225g (8 oz) Cheshire cheese,
  sliced

2 tablespoons chopped fresh
  marjoram
1 tablespoon snipped chives
4 rashers back bacon, rinds
  removed
150ml (¼ pint) double cream

Roll out two-thirds of the prepared pastry on a lightly-floured
surface to a round large enough to line a 20-cm (8-inch) loose-
bottomed shallow sandwich tin or deep flan tin (see page 54).
Line the base with half of the potatoes and season generously.

146

Top with the cheese and herbs. Arrange the bacon on top of the herbs. Top with the remaining potatoes. Pour over the cream, reserving 2 tablespoons.

Roll out the remaining pastry to make a lid. Dampen the pastry rim with water and cover with the lid. Trim, seal and flute the edges. Make a small hole in the pie crust to allow the escape of steam. Brush with the reserved cream to glaze and use any pastry trimmings to decorate the pie as liked.

Place on a baking tray and cook in a preheated hot oven (220°C, 425°F, Gas Mark 7) for 25 minutes. Reduce the oven temperature to moderately hot (190°C, 375°F, Gas Mark 5) and cook for a further 10–15 minutes. Cover the top with a little foil to prevent over-browning if necessary. Serve hot or cold, cut into wedges.

Individual Pork and Pippin Pies

Serves 4

1 tablespoon oil
450g (1 lb) boneless tenderloin
  pork, cut into bite-sized
  pieces
1 tablespoon flour
300ml (½ pint) unsweetened
  apple juice or dry cider
300ml (½ pint) chicken stock
salt and freshly ground black
  pepper

½ teaspoon dried sage
4 Cox's Orange Pippin apples,
  peeled, cored and thickly
  sliced
½ quantity Rough Puff Pastry
  (see page 28)
beaten egg to glaze

Heat the oil in a saucepan. Add the pork and cook over a moderate heat for about 15 minutes until well browned. Add the flour and cook for 1 minute. Gradually add the apple juice or cider and chicken stock, stirring well. Season generously and stir in the sage. Cook for 10 minutes then spoon into four individual pie dishes and leave to cool slightly. Top each pie filling with an equal quantity of apple slices.

Roll out the prepared pastry on a lightly-floured surface and cut into four rounds about 4cm (1½ inches) larger than the pie dishes. Trim a 2.5-cm (1-inch) strip from each and use to line the dampened rims of each dish. Dampen the pastry rims with water and cover with the lids (see page 50). Trim, seal and flute the edges. Use any pastry trimmings to decorate the pies as liked.

Brush with beaten egg to glaze and cook in a preheated moderately hot oven (190°C, 375°F, Gas Mark 5) for 30 minutes until well-risen, golden brown and cooked through. Serve hot.

Egg and Chicken Bake Pie

Serves 4

50g (2 oz) butter
1 onion, peeled and chopped
100g (4 oz) button mushrooms,
  chopped
225g (8 oz) cooked chicken, cut
  into bite-sized pieces
4 tomatoes, peeled, seeds
  removed and chopped
4 hard-boiled eggs, sliced
25g (1 oz) plain flour

300ml (½ pint) chicken stock
1 egg yolk
1 tablespoon chopped fresh
  parsley
1 teaspoon dried tarragon
salt and freshly ground black
  pepper
¼ quantity Puff Pastry (see
  page 25)
beaten egg to glaze

Melt 25g (1 oz) of the butter in a large saucepan. Add the onion
and mushrooms and cook until softened, about 5–8 minutes.
Mix with the chicken, tomato and sliced eggs. Place in a
medium-sized pie dish.

Melt the remaining butter in a saucepan. Add the flour and
cook for 1 minute. Gradually add the chicken stock and cook for
3 minutes, stirring. Remove from the heat, add the egg yolk,
parsley, tarragon and seasoning to taste. Pour over the chicken
mixture and allow to cool slightly.

Roll out the prepared pastry on a lightly-floured surface to a
round about 4cm (1½ inches) larger than the pie dish. Trim a
2.5-cm (1-inch) strip from the edge of the pastry and use to line
the dampened rim of the dish. Dampen the pastry rim with
water and cover with the lid (see page 50). Trim, seal and flute
the edges. Use any pastry trimmings to decorate the pie as
liked.

Brush with beaten egg to glaze and cook in a preheated
moderately hot oven (200°C, 400°F, Gas Mark 6) for 25–30
minutes until well-risen, golden brown and cooked through.

Mid-week Herby Sausage and Egg Pie

Serves 4-6

1½ quantities Shortcrust
  Pastry (see page 12)
3 hard-boiled eggs
225g (8 oz) herb-flavoured
  sausagemeat
2 eggs, beaten

150ml (¼ pint) single cream or
  milk
1 teaspoon dried sage
salt and freshly ground black
  pepper

Roll out two-thirds of the prepared pastry on a lightly-floured
surface to a round large enough to line a 20-cm (8-inch) flan ring

set on a greased baking tray (see page 54).

Halve the eggs lengthwise and place on the pastry base, yolk side down. Top with the sausagemeat, moulding it around the eggs. Mix almost all the beaten egg with the cream or milk, sage and seasoning to taste. Pour over the sausagemeat.

Roll out the remaining pastry to make a lid. Dampen the pastry rim with water and cover with the lid. Trim, seal and flute the edges. Use any pastry trimmings to decorate the pie as liked.

Brush with beaten egg to glaze and cook in a preheated moderate oven (160°C, 325°F, Gas Mark 3) for about 1 hour until golden-brown and cooked through. Serve hot or cold, cut into wedges.

Scottish Supper Pies

Serves 6

FILLING
450g (1 lb) lamb shoulder, cut into 1-cm (½-inch) cubes
25g (1 oz) plain flour
2 teaspoons dry mustard powder
salt and freshly ground black pepper
25g (1 oz) meat dripping or butter

3 leeks, trimmed and sliced
3 carrots, peeled and chopped
250ml (8 fl oz) beer
PASTRY
275g (10 oz) plain flour
150g (5 oz) meat dripping or butter
4-5 tablespoons cold water
beaten egg to glaze

Prepare the filling: toss the meat with the flour, mustard powder and seasoning to taste. Melt the dripping or butter in a saucepan. Add the meat and fry until browned on all sides. Add the leek, carrot and any remaining flour. Cook for 2–3 minutes then gradually add the beer. Cover and cook over a gentle heat for 40 minutes. Allow to cool.

Line six greased deep individual pie dishes or soufflé dishes with greased foil.

Prepare the pastry: sift the flour into a mixing bowl. Cut the dripping or butter in small pieces and rub into the flour until the mixture resembles fine breadcrumbs. Bind to a stiff dough with the water. Roll out two-thirds of the pastry on a lightly-floured surface and cut out six round bases and lids for the prepared dishes. Place the bases in the dishes. Fill with the meat mixture. Dampen the pastry rims with water and cover with the lids, sealing well. Use any pastry trimmings to decorate the pies as liked.

Brush with beaten egg to glaze and cook in a preheated moderately hot oven (190°C, 375°F, Gas Mark 5) for 35–40 minutes until the pastry is crisp and golden. Serve hot with fresh vegetables in season or cold with salads.

Curried Farmhouse Pies

Makes 4

25g (1 oz) butter or margarine
1 small onion, peeled and
  chopped
2 sticks celery, chopped
1 tablespoon flour
150ml (¼ pint) milk
175g (6 oz) cooked chicken,
  chopped

1 (225-g/8-oz) can curried
  beans with sultanas
salt
1 quantity Shortcrust Pastry
  (see page 12)

Melt the butter or margarine in a saucepan. Add the onion and celery and fry until soft and translucent. Stir in the flour and cook for 1 minute. Gradually add the milk, stirring to make a smooth sauce. Cook for 1 minute then allow to cool. Stir in the chicken and beans and season to taste with salt.

Roll out the pastry on a lightly-floured surface and cut out four bases and lids to fit four individual pie or Yorkshire pudding tins. Place the bases in the tins and fill with the bean mixture. Dampen the pastry rims with water and cover with the lids. Trim, seal and flute the edges. Make a small cut in the top of each pie to allow any steam to escape during cooking.

Cook in a preheated moderately hot oven (200°C, 400°F, Gas Mark 6) for 25–30 minutes until golden brown and cooked through. Serve warm or cold.

Olde English Turkey Pie

Serves 6

1½ quantities Shortcrust
  Pastry (see page 12)
FILLING
225g (8 oz) pork sausagemeat
2 tablespoons dry cider
1 teaspoon mixed dried herbs
3 tablespoons chopped fresh
  parsley
3 hard-boiled eggs, sliced
350g (12 oz) cooked turkey,
  chopped

1 small leek, finely sliced
1 onion, peeled and chopped
¼ teaspoon ground nutmeg
salt and freshly ground black
  pepper
beaten egg to glaze
JELLY
300ml (½ pint) dry cider
2 teaspoons vinegar
2 teaspoons powdered gelatine

Roll out two-thirds of the prepared pastry on a lightly-floured surface to a round large enough to line a 20-cm (8-inch) sandwich tin or deep pie plate (see page 00).

Prepare the filling: mix the sausagemeat with the cider, dried herbs and parsley, blending well. Spread over the base of the pie. Top with a layer of egg, turkey, leek and onion. Sprinkle with the nutmeg and seasoning to taste.

Roll out the remaining pastry to make a lid. Dampen the pastry rim with water and cover with the lid. Trim, seal and flute the edges. Use any pastry trimmings to decorate the pie as liked.

Brush with beaten egg to glaze and cook in a preheated hot oven (220°C, 425°F, Gas Mark 7) for 30 minutes. Reduce the oven temperature to moderate (160°C, 325°F, Gas Mark 3) and cook for a further 30 minutes. Allow to cool slightly in the tin before turning out onto a wire rack to cool completely.

Prepare the jelly: place the cider and vinegar in a small pan. Sprinkle over the gelatine and leave to soften, about 5 minutes. Heat gently until clear and dissolved. Allow to cool but not set.

Make a small hole in the pie crust and carefully pour the thickened jelly into the pie. Chill to set. Serve cold, cut into thick wedges, with salad.

Anglesey Pie

Serves 4

25g (1 oz) butter	*225g (8 oz) cooked chicken,*
25g (1 oz) flour	*chopped*
150ml (¼ pint) milk	*3 leeks, sliced*
150ml (¼ pint) dry white wine	*2 hard-boiled eggs, sliced*
salt and freshly ground black	*1 quantity Shortcrust Pastry*
pepper	*(see page 12)*
1 tablespoon chopped fresh	*beaten egg to glaze*
parsley	

Melt the butter in a saucepan. Add the flour and cook for 1 minute. Gradually add the milk and wine, stirring to keep the sauce smooth. Bring to the boil and cook for 1 minute. Season to taste. Remove from the heat and stir in the parsley, chicken, leeks and eggs. Spoon into a medium-sized pie dish.

Roll out the prepared pastry on a lightly-floured surface to a round about 4 cm (1½ inches) larger than the pie dish. Trim a 2.5-cm (1-inch) strip from the edge of the pastry and use to line the dampened rim of the dish. Dampen the pastry rim with water and cover with the lid (see page 50). Trim, seal and flute the edges. Use any pastry trimmings to decorate the pie as liked.

Brush with beaten egg to glaze and cook in a preheated moderately hot oven (190°C, 375°F, Gas Mark 5) for about 1 hour until the pastry is crisp and golden brown.

Sausage Fidget Pie

Serves 4

2 medium potatoes, peeled and
  sliced
2 cooking apples, peeled, cored
  and sliced
450g (1 lb) pork sausages,
  halved
1 large onion, peeled and
  sliced
1 tablespoon brown sugar
2 tablespoons made mild
  English mustard

1 teaspoon dried sage
1 teaspoon chopped fresh
  parsley
salt and freshly ground black
  pepper
150ml (¼ pint) water
1 quantity Herby Shortcrust
  Pastry (see page 13)
beaten egg to glaze

Place the potato slices in the base of a 1.2-litre (2-pint) pie dish.
Top with the apple, sausages and onion. Sprinkle with the
sugar. Mix the mustard with the sage, parsley and seasoning to
taste and blend in the water. Pour over the pie filling.

Roll out the prepared pastry on a lightly-floured surface to a
round about 4cm (1½ inches) larger than the pie dish. Trim a
2.5-cm (1-inch) strip from the edge of the pastry and use to line
the dampened rim of the dish. Dampen the pastry rim with
water and cover with the lid (see page 50). Trim, seal and flute
the edges. Use any pastry trimmings to decorate the pie as
liked.

Brush with beaten egg to glaze and cook in a preheated hot
oven (230°C, 450°F, Gas Mark 8) for 30 minutes. Reduce the
oven temperature to cool (150°C, 300°F, Gas Mark 2) and cook
for a further 45 minutes.

Minced Meat and Egg Pie

Serves 4

15g (½ oz) butter
1 onion, peeled and chopped
450g (1 lb) pork, minced
150g (5 oz) streaky bacon,
  rind removed and chopped
15g (½ oz) plain flour
1 teaspoon chopped fresh
  tarragon

150ml (¼ pint) chicken stock
3 hard-boiled eggs, halved
  lengthways
1 quantity Onion Pastry (see
  page 20)
beaten egg to glaze
1 teaspoon onion salt
  (optional)

Melt the butter in a saucepan. Add the onion and cook until soft
but not brown. Drain off any excess fat and stir in the pork and
bacon. Cook over a moderate heat until well browned. Drain off

any excess fat and add the flour. Mix well and cook for 1 minute. Add the tarragon and chicken stock. Place half of the mixture in a 1.2-litre (2-pint) pie dish with a pie funnel. Place the egg halves in a circle on top. Top with the remaining meat mixture.

Roll out the prepared pastry on a lightly-floured surface to a round about 4cm (1½ inches) larger than the pie dish. Trim a 2.5-cm (1-inch) strip from the edge of the pastry and use to line the dampened rim of the dish. Dampen the pastry rim with water and cover with the lid (see page 50). Trim, seal and flute the edges. Use any pastry trimmings to decorate the pie as liked.

Brush with beaten egg to glaze and sprinkle with the onion salt, if used. Cook in a preheated moderately hot oven (200°C, 400°F, Gas Mark 6) for 35–40 minutes until golden brown. Serve hot with vegetables in season.

Crusty Lamb Pies

Serves 4

675g (1½ lb) scrag lamb	*1 onion, peeled and chopped*
1 bay leaf	*1 potato, peeled and chopped*
salt and freshly ground black	*1 quantity Hot Water Crust*
pepper	*Pastry (see page 39)*
1 carrot, peeled and chopped	*beaten egg to glaze*

Place the lamb in a saucepan with the bay leaf and seasoning to taste. Cover with water and bring to the boil. Simmer for 45 minutes. Add the carrot, onion and potato. Cover and simmer for 10 minutes. Remove the meat and vegetables with a slotted spoon and fork the meat away from the bones. Discard the bones and reserve the cooking liquor.

Roll out the prepared pastry on a lightly-floured surface and cut out four round bases and lids to fit four individual pie or Yorkshire pudding tins. Place the bases in the tins and divide the meat evenly between the pies. Add 1 teaspoon reserved liquor to each pie. Dampen the pastry rims with water and cover with the lids. Trim and flute the edges decoratively. Use any pastry trimmings to decorate the pies as liked.

Brush with beaten egg to glaze and cook in a preheated moderately hot oven (200°C, 400°F, Gas Mark 6) for 30 minutes until golden brown and cooked through. Serve with vegetables in season.

Prince of Wales Turkey Pie

Serves 12

PASTRY
675g (1½ lb) plain flour
1½ teaspoons salt
175g (6 oz) lard
200ml (7 fl oz) water
150ml (¼ pint) milk
beaten egg to glaze

FILLING
350g (12 oz) streaky bacon,
  rinds removed and minced
1 onion, peeled and minced
350g (12 oz) pork sausagemeat

1 teaspoon dried thyme
¼ teaspoon ground nutmeg
salt and freshly ground black
  pepper
675g (1½ lb) raw boneless
  turkey meat
8 small hard-boiled eggs

JELLY
150ml (¼ pint) chicken or
  turkey stock
150ml (¼ pint) cider
15g (½ oz) powdered gelatine

Prepare the pastry: sift the flour and salt into a mixing bowl. Place the lard, water and milk in a saucepan and heat gently until the lard melts then bring to the boil. Pour at once into the flour and mix to form a pliable dough. Knead lightly on a lightly floured surface until smooth and free from cracks. Roll out three-quarters of the pastry and use to line the base and sides of a greased 25-cm (10-inch) loose-bottomed round cake tin or pie mould (see page 52). Keep the remaining dough covered and warm while filling the pie.

Prepare the filling: mix the bacon with the onion, sausage-meat, thyme, nutmeg and seasoning to taste, blending well. Remove any skin from the turkey and cut the meat into small pieces. Mix with the sausagemeat mixture, mixing well.

Place half of the meat mixture in the pastry-lined tin and make eight small indentations for the eggs. Position the eggs in the indentations and cover with the remaining meat mixture.

Roll out the remaining pastry to make a lid. Dampen the pastry rim with water and cover with the lid. Trim, seal and flute the edges attractively. Use any pastry trimmings to decorate the pie – Prince of Wales feathers are the traditional decoration. Make several holes in the pie crust to allow any steam to escape during cooking.

Brush with beaten egg to glaze and stand the pie on a baking tray. Cook in a preheated moderately hot oven (200°C, 400°F, Gas Mark 6) for 45 minutes. Reduce the oven temperature to moderate (160°C, 325°F, Gas Mark 3), brush the pie again with beaten egg and cook for a further 1½ hours. If the pie starts to brown too much then cover the crust with a sheet of greaseproof paper. When cooked, remove from the oven and allow to cool in the tin.

Meanwhile, place the stock and cider in a small pan. Sprinkle over the gelatine and leave to soak for about 5 minutes to soften.

Heat slowly until clear and dissolved. Allow to cool slightly then pour into the pie through the holes in the crust. Leave until quite cold then chill. Serve the pie cold, cut into thick wedges, with salads.

Pork and Bacon Picnic Pie

Serves 6–8

1 quantity Hot Water Crust Pastry (see page 39)
450g (1 lb) slipper joint bacon, soaked overnight and chopped
350g (12 oz) shoulder pork, chopped
2 tablespoons finely chopped fresh parsley

grated rind and juice of ½ lemon
½ teaspoon salt
freshly ground black pepper
beaten egg to glaze
300ml (½ pint) aspic jelly
lemon slices to garnish

Roll out three-quarters of the prepared pastry and use to line the base and sides of a 1-kg (2-lb) loaf tin. Allow the pastry to cover the top edge of the tin (see page 52).

Mix the bacon with the pork, parsley, lemon rind, lemon juice and seasoning to taste. Spoon into the pastry-lined tin.

Roll out the reserved pastry on a lightly-floured surface to a long strip, 2.5cm (1 inch) wide and 60cm (24 inches) long. Cut the strip into three equal portions crosswise. Dampen the pastry rim with water and attach the three strips to one of the shorter edges of the tin. Plait the strips together and then attach to the pastry rim at the other shorter end of the pie. Seal the edges on the longer sides of the tin. Trim all the edges neatly and flute if liked.

Brush with beaten egg to glaze and cook in a preheated hot oven (230°C, 450°F, Gas Mark 8) for 15 minutes then reduce the oven temperature to moderate (160°C, 325°F, Gas Mark 3) and cook for a further 2¼ hours. Cover the pie with foil to prevent over-browning if necessary. Allow to cool in the tin.

When quite cold, make a small hole in the pie crust and pour in the aspic jelly through a small funnel. Reserve a little of the jelly to set the lemon slices in a decorative pattern on the crust of the pie. Chill to set. Serve the pie sliced with salad.

Bacon and Apple Raised Pie

Serves 6–8

*1 quantity Hot Water Crust
  Pastry (see page 39)
1kg (2 lb) collar bacon, cooked
  and chopped
2 tablespoons finely chopped
  fresh parsley
100g (4 oz) fresh white
  breadcrumbs
1 egg, beaten*

*150ml (¼ pint) milk
1 small eating apple, cored
  and finely chopped
1 onion, peeled and finely
  chopped
50g (2 oz) raisins
salt and freshly ground black
  pepper
beaten egg to glaze*

Roll out two-thirds of the prepared pastry on a lightly-floured surface and use to line the base and sides of a greased hinged pie tin measuring 21 × 7.5 × 7.5cm (8½ × 3 × 3 inches) or a loose-bottomed 13-cm (5-inch) round cake tin (see page 66).

Mix the bacon with the parsley, breadcrumbs, egg, milk, apple, onion, raisins and seasoning to taste. Spoon into the pastry-lined tin. Roll out the remaining pastry to make a lid. Dampen the pastry rim with water and cover with the lid. Trim, seal and flute the edges. Use any pastry trimmings to decorate the pie as liked.

Brush with beaten egg to glaze and cook in a preheated moderately hot oven (200°C, 400°F, Gas Mark 6) for 30 minutes, then reduce the oven temperature to moderate (160°C, 325°F, Gas Mark 3) and cook for a further 2¾–3 hours. Allow to cool in the tin. Slice to serve.

PIZZAS AND PÂTÉS

Bacon and Mushroom Pizza

Serves 2–4

½ quantity Pizza Dough (see
  page 46)
225g (8 oz) streaky bacon,
  rinds removed and chopped
100g (4 oz) mushrooms, sliced
1 onion, peeled and sliced
3 tomatoes, peeled and sliced

½ teaspoon dried oregano
1 tablespoon finely chopped
  fresh parsley
salt and freshly ground black
  pepper
100g (4 oz) Cheddar or
  Gruyère cheese, grated

Roll out the prepared pastry on a lightly-floured surface to a 23-cm (9-inch) round and place in a pizza pan or on a baking tray. Cover with polythene or cling film and leave in a warm place to prove while making the topping.

Place the bacon in a pan with the mushrooms, onion, tomatoes, oregano, parsley and seasoning to taste. Cook over a low heat until the mixture is softened and cooked. Increase the heat and cook until the mixture is dry. Remove from the heat and allow to cool.

Place the cooled filling on top of the pizza base and top with the cheese. Cook in a preheated hot oven (230°C, 450°F, Gas Mark 8) for 25 minutes until well-risen, golden brown and cooked through. Serve cut into wedges.

Ratatouille Pan Pizza

Serves 4

175g (6 oz) self-raising flour
pinch of salt
25g (1 oz) butter
about 90ml (3 fl oz) water
2 tablespoons oil

1 (425-g/15-oz) can ratatouille
75g (3 oz) Cheddar cheese,
  grated

10 black olives

Sift the flour and salt into a mixing bowl. Rub in the butter until the mixture resembles fine breadcrumbs. Add the water and mix to a soft dough. Roll out on a lightly-floured surface to a 25-cm (10-inch) round.

Heat the oil in a heavy-based 25-cm (10-inch) frying pan. Add the pizza base and fry gently until golden on one side, about 5 minutes. Turn over with a spatula. Top with the ratatouille and sprinkle with the cheese. Top with the olives and cook for about 7 minutes until the second side is golden brown. Brown under a preheated hot grill for 2–3 minutes until hot and bubbly. Serve hot, cut in wedges, straight from the pan.

Smoked Mackerel Pâté en Croûte

Serves 6

50g (2 oz) butter
350g (12 oz) smoked mackerel,
skinned and flesh flaked
2 tablespoons lemon juice
175g (6 oz) cream cheese
1 egg
freshly ground black pepper
¾ quantity Shortcrust Pastry
(see page 12)

2 canned pimientos, chopped
50g (2 oz) capers, coarsely
chopped
3 tablespoons chopped fresh
parsley
beaten egg to glaze

Melt the butter in a saucepan. Add the flaked mackerel and cook gently for 2–3 minutes. Add the lemon juice, cream cheese, egg and pepper to taste. Allow to cool.

Roll out three-quarters of the prepared pastry on a lightly-floured surface to a rectangle large enough to line a 750-ml (1¼-pint) oblong foil loaf dish or small loaf tin (see page 85). Place a layer of pimiento on the pastry base and top with the capers. Cover with half of the mackerel mixture. Sprinkle over the parsley then cover with the remaining fish mixture. Roll out the remaining pastry to make a lid. Dampen the pastry rim with water and cover with the lid. Trim, seal and flute the edges. Use any pastry trimmings to decorate the pastry as liked.

Brush with beaten egg to glaze and cook in a preheated moderately hot oven (200°C, 400°F, Gas Mark 6) for about 40 minutes. Cool then chill before slicing to serve.

Chicken Galantine in a Crust

Serves 6–8

*1 (1.5-kg/3-lb) boiling chicken,
  skinned*
1 tablespoon tomato purée
*1 teaspoon freshly ground
  black pepper*
1 teaspoon dried tarragon
1 teaspoon soy sauce
*1 teaspoon Worcestershire
  sauce*
1 egg, beaten

120ml (4 fl oz) dry white wine
salt to taste
*675g (1½ lb) piece streaky
  bacon, rind removed*
2 bay leaves
*½ quantity Puff or 1 quantity
  Rough Puff Pastry
  (see pages 25 and 28)*
beaten egg to glaze

With a sharp knife, remove all the flesh from the chicken. Mince coarsely and mix with the tomato purée, pepper, tarragon, soy and Worcestershire sauces, egg, wine and salt to taste. Divide the mixture in half. Place one half on a greased sheet of foil and shape into an oblong about 5mm (¼ inch) thick.

Cut the bacon into long strips and arrange them lengthways on the chicken oblong. Cover with the rest of the chicken mixture to completely enclose. Place the bay leaves on top and roll up like a Swiss roll, using the foil to lift the mixture. Completely enclose in the foil, twisting the ends to seal and steam over a gentle heat for 3 hours.

Weight and allow to cool overnight. Remove the foil and bay leaves.

Divide the prepared pastry in half. Roll out each piece on a lightly-floured surface to a rectangle large enough to cover the galantine. Place the galantine on one pastry rectangle. Brush the pastry edges with beaten egg and cover with the second pastry rectangle. Seal the edges carefully and flute attractively. Use any pastry trimmings to decorate the top of the galantine as liked.

Brush with beaten egg to glaze. Place on a dampened baking tray and cook in a preheated hot oven (220°C, 425°F, Gas Mark 7) for 30–45 minutes until the pastry is well-risen and golden. Serve hot or cold, cut into slices.

Duck Pâté in Pastry

Serves 8

2 quantities Rich Shortcrust
  Blender Pastry (see page 15)
225g (8 oz) belly of pork,
  minced
1 (1.8-kg/4-lb) duck, boned
  and chopped
225g (8 oz) pork fillet, chopped
225g (8 oz) chicken livers,
  chopped
1 egg, beaten

1 clove garlic, peeled and
  crushed
2 tablespoons brandy
1 teaspoon mixed dried herbs
pinch of mixed spice
pinch of ground allspice
grated rind of 1 orange
salt and freshly ground black
  pepper
beaten egg to glaze

Roll out three-quarters of the prepared pastry on a lightly-floured surface to a rectangle large enough to line a 20-cm (8-inch) hinged, rectangular raised pie mould (see page 85).

Mix the pork with the duck, pork fillet, chicken livers, beaten egg, garlic, brandy, herbs, spices, orange rind and seasoning to taste. Spoon into the pastry-lined mould and level the surface.

Roll out the remaining pastry to make a lid. Brush the pastry edges with beaten egg and cover with the lid, sealing the edges carefully. Brush with beaten egg to glaze. Use any pastry trimmings to decorate the pastry as liked and make a small hole in the crust to allow any steam to escape during cooking.

Cook in a preheated moderately hot oven (200°C, 400°F, Gas Mark 6) for 20 minutes. Reduce the oven temperature to moderate (160°C, 325°F, Gas Mark 3) and cook for a further 1¾-2 hours until the pâté is cooked. Test with a fine skewer. Cover the crust with a piece of foil to prevent over-browning if necessary. Allow to cool thoroughly before serving cut into slices.

SWEET QUICHES, TARTS AND FLANS

Apricot, Mace and Almond Tart

Serves 6

PASTRY
175g (6 oz) plain flour
1 teaspoon ground mace
75g (3 oz) butter or margarine
cold water to bind

FILLING
450g (1 lb) apricots, peeled,
halved and stoned or 1
(822-g/1 lb 13-oz) can
apricot halves, well drained

100g (4 oz) butter
100g (4 oz) castor sugar
100g (4 oz) ground almonds
1 teaspoon ground mace
2 eggs, beaten

TOPPING
175g (6 oz) icing sugar, sifted
2 tablespoons lemon juice
2 tablespoons apricot jam,
warmed

Prepare the pastry: sift the flour and mace into a mixing bowl. Cut the butter or margarine into small pieces and rub into the flour until the mixture resembles fine breadcrumbs. Add sufficient cold water to bind to a firm but pliable dough. Roll out on a lightly-floured surface to a round large enough to line a 20-cm (8-inch) flan tin (see page 54).

Prepare the filling: arrange the apricot halves, cut-sides down, in the base of the dish, reserving a few for decoration. Beat the butter with the sugar until light and fluffy. Add the almonds, mace and eggs, mixing well to blend. Carefully spread the mixture over the apricots to completely cover.

Cook in a preheated moderate oven (180°C, 350°F, Gas Mark 4) for 50–60 minutes until well-risen, golden and firm to the touch. Allow to cool.

When cool, mix the icing sugar with the lemon juice to make a smooth glacé icing. Spread evenly over the cold tart. Decorate with the reserved apricot halves. Brush the apricot halves with apricot jam to glaze. Allow the icing to set before serving cut into wedges.

Individual Rhubarb Crumbles

Makes 24

1 quantity Pâté Sucrée
  (see page 21)
450g (1 lb) rhubarb
sugar to taste
CRUMBLE TOPPING
75g (3 oz) plain flour

15g (½ oz) porridge oats
75g (3 oz) demerara sugar
50g (2 oz) butter, melted

Roll out the prepared pastry on a lightly-floured surface and cut out twenty-four (7.5-cm/3-inch) rounds with a fluted scone or biscuit cutter. Fit into greased patty tins and chill while preparing the filling.

Trim the rhubarb and cut into 2.5-cm (1-inch) lengths. Place in a saucepan with 2–3 tablespoons water and sugar to taste, about 40g (1½ oz). Cook gently until softened, about 5–8 minutes. Allow to cool.

Prepare the crumble topping: mix the flour with the porridge oats and demerara sugar. Pour over the melted butter and mix in with a fork to give a crumble mixture.

Divide the rhubarb between the pastry cases. Top with the crumble mixture and cook in a preheated moderately hot oven (200°C, 400°F, Gas Mark 6) for about 35 minutes until browned and cooked through. Serve hot or cold.

Individual Loganberry Tarts

Makes 12

½ quantity Pâté Sucré
  the flour (see page 21)
1 (425-g/15-oz) can
  loganberries

2 teaspoons arrowroot powder
150ml (¼ pint) soured cream
ground nutmeg to dust

Roll out the prepared pastry on a lightly-floured surface and cut out twelve (7.5-cm/3-inch) rounds with a fluted scone or biscuit cutter. Fit into greased patty tins. Prick the bases with a fork and bake 'blind' in a preheated moderately hot oven (200°C, 400°F, Gas Mark 6) for 10–15 minutes (see page 58). Remove the beans or foil and allow to cool on a wire rack.

Drain the juice from the loganberries and place in a saucepan with the arrowroot powder. Bring to the boil, stirring constantly, until clear and thickened. Allow to cool slightly.

Divide the loganberries between the pastry cases and spoon over the cooled glaze. Allow to set. Just before serving, top each tart with a swirl of soured cream and dust with ground nutmeg.

Rhubarb and Coriander Crumble Tart

Serves 4-6

PASTRY
225g (8 oz) plain flour
175g (6 oz) butter
75g (3 oz) castor sugar
1 egg yolk, beaten
cold water to bind

FILLING
450g (1 lb) rhubarb, trimmed
and finely sliced

100g (4 oz) ground almonds
100g (4 oz) demerara sugar
1 tablespoon ground coriander

TO SERVE
150ml (¼ pint) double cream
1 teaspoon ground coriander

Prepare the pastry: sift the flour into a mixing bowl. Cut the butter into small pieces and rub into the flour until the mixture resembles fine breadcrumbs. Add the sugar and mix well to blend. Add the egg yolk and sufficient cold water to bind to a firm but pliable dough. Chill lightly. Roll out on a lightly-floured surface to a round large enough to line a deep 20-cm (8-inch) flan tin (see page 54).

Prepare the filling: arrange the rhubarb in the base of the tin, packing well together. Mix the almonds with the sugar and coriander. Sprinkle this mixture evenly over the top of the rhubarb. Cook in a preheated moderate oven (160°C, 325°F, Gas Mark 3) for 1 hour until golden and cooked.

Meanwhile, whip the cream with the coriander until it stands in soft peaks. Serve the tart slightly warm with the cream.

Almond and Spice Greengage Tart

Serves 4-6

PASTRY
100g (4 oz) plain flour
100g (4 oz) butter
50g (2 oz) ground almonds
½ teaspoon ground mixed
  spice
¼ teaspoon finely grated
  lemon rind
50g (2 oz) castor sugar
1 egg yolk

FILLING
50g (2 oz) castor sugar
25g (1 oz) ground almonds
675g (1½ lb) greengages,
  stoned
5 tablespoons greengage,
  gooseberry or apricot jam
2 tablespoons lemon juice
15g (½ oz) flaked almonds

Prepare the pastry: sift the flour into a mixing bowl. Cut the butter into small pieces and rub into the flour until the mixture resembles fine breadcrumbs. Stir in the almonds, mixed spice, lemon rind and castor sugar. Add the egg yolk and bind to make a firm but pliable dough. Wrap in greaseproof paper or cling film and chill for 1 hour.

Roll out on a lightly-floured surface to a round large enough to line a 20-cm (8-inch) flan dish or ring set on a baking tray (see page 54).

Prepare the filling: mix the castor sugar and ground almonds together and place on the base of the pastry case. Top with the greengages. Cook in a preheated moderate oven (180°C, 350°F, Gas Mark 4) for 35–40 minutes until golden and cooked through.

Meanwhile, heat the jam with the lemon juice until syrupy. Sieve then spoon over the tart. Sprinkle with the flaked almonds and allow to cool. Serve warm or cold with whipped cream.

Glazed Raspberry Flan

Serves 6

PASTRY
175g (6 oz) plain flour
75g (3 oz) butter
40g (1½ oz) castor sugar
2 egg yolks
3 teaspoons cold water
FILLING
25g (1 oz) butter
25g (1 oz) plain flour
300ml (½ pint) milk

25g (1 oz) castor sugar
1 egg yolk
1 tablespoon single cream
1 tablespoon sweet sherry
  (optional)
TOPPING
350g (12 oz) raspberries, hulled
4 tablespoons seedless
  raspberry jam
1 tablespoon lemon juice

Prepare the pastry: sift the flour into a mixing bowl. Cut the butter into small pieces and rub into the flour until the mixture resembles fine breadcrumbs. Stir in the sugar and mix well to blend. Mix the egg yolks and water together and mix into the mixture. Form into a firm dough.

Roll out on a lightly-floured surface to a round large enough to line a 20-cm (8-inch) flan tin (see page 54). Bake 'blind' in a preheated moderately hot oven (200°C, 400°F, Gas Mark 6) for 15-20 minutes (see page 54). Remove the foil or beans and bake for a further 5-10 minutes or until cooked. Allow to cool on a wire rack.

Prepare the filling: melt the butter in a saucepan. Add the flour and cook for 1 minute. Gradually add the milk and bring to the boil, stirring constantly. Allow to cool slightly then add the sugar, egg yolk, cream and sherry, if used. Pour into the pastry case and allow to cool.

Arrange the raspberries over the cool filling. Prepare the glaze by heating the jam with the lemon juice until well mixed. Spoon over the raspberries and leave to cool and set. Chill before serving with whipped cream.

Gooseberry Lattice Tart

Serves 4-6

450g (1 lb) gooseberries, topped and tailed	*1 tablespoon ground rice*
	2 tablespoons water
grated rind and juice of ½ orange	*1 quantity Orange Shortcrust Pastry (see page 13)*
50g (2 oz) sugar	*beaten egg to glaze*

Place the gooseberries in a saucepan with the orange rind, orange juice and sugar. Cook gently, over a low heat, until just tender. Blend the ground rice with the water, stir into the fruit and cook gently, stirring very lightly until thickened. Allow to cool.

Roll out two-thirds of the prepared pastry on a lightly-floured surface to a round large enough to line a 23-cm (9-inch) pie plate (see page 50). Fill with the cold fruit mixture. Roll out the remaining pastry and cut out twelve strips for the lattice. Brush the edge of the pastry case with beaten egg and lay on the first six strips of pastry. Brush with the beaten egg then lattice with the remaining six strips of pastry (see page 94). Brush the lattice again with beaten egg to glaze. Cook in a preheated hot oven (220°C, 425°F, Gas Mark 7) for 25 minutes until golden brown.

Apple and Pear Sugar-crusted Flan

Serves 4-6

PASTRY
150g (5 oz) plain flour
pinch of salt
75g (3 oz) butter
15g (½ oz) castor sugar
1 egg, beaten
FILLING
2 tablespoons custard powder
600ml (1 pint) milk

75g (3 oz) spaghetti rings
15g (½ oz) castor sugar
100g (4 oz) sliced cooking
  apples
100g (4 oz) sliced cooking
  pears
lemon juice to brush
50g (2 oz) demerara sugar
1 teaspoon ground cinnamon

Prepare the pastry: sift the flour and salt into a mixing bowl. Cut the butter into small pieces and rub into the flour until the mixture resembles fine breadcrumbs. Stir in the sugar, mixing well. Bind with the beaten egg to a firm but pliable dough.

Roll out on a lightly-floured surface to a round large enough to line a 20-cm (8-inch) flan ring set on a greased baking tray (see page 54). Bake 'blind' in a preheated moderately hot oven (200°C, 400°F, Gas Mark 6) for 15 minutes until golden (see page 54). Remove the foil or beans.

Prepare the filling: mix the custard powder to a smooth paste with some of the milk. Bring the remaining milk to the boil, add the spaghetti rings and cook for 8 minutes. Carefully add the custard powder, mixing well and cook until thickened, about 2 minutes. Add the sugar and pour into the pastry case.

Place the apple and pear slices decoratively on top of the pasta and custard filling and brush with lemon juice. Mix the demerara sugar with the cinnamon and sprinkle over the flan. Cook in a preheated moderate oven (180°C, 350°F, Gas Mark 4) for about 20 minutes until golden. Serve with cream if liked.

Pear and Frangipane Tart

Serves 4-6

1 quantity Pâte Sucrée
  (see page 21)
3-4 ripe dessert pears
350g (12 oz) sugar
300ml (½ pint) water
1 vanilla pod or a few drops of
  vanilla essence
FRANGIPANE
100g (4 oz) butter
100g (4 oz) castor sugar

2 eggs
100g (4 oz) ground almonds
25g (1 oz) flour
almond essence or kirsch to
  flavour
GLAZE
6 tablespoons apricot jam
2 tablespoons water
whipped cream or pistachio
  nuts to decorate

Roll out the prepared pastry on a lightly-floured surface to a round large enough to line a 20-cm (8-inch) flan tin (see page 54). Prick the base with a fork.

Meanwhile, peel, halve and core the pears. Boil the sugar with the water and vanilla. Add the pears and poach until tender, about 20–25 minutes. Remove with a slotted spoon and cool.

Prepare the frangipane: beat the butter with the sugar. Beat in the eggs, a little at a time, then stir in the almonds, flour and almond essence or kirsch to taste.

Fill the pastry case with the frangipane and cook in a preheated moderately hot oven (190°C, 375°F, Gas Mark 5) for about 25 minutes until cooked through. Allow to cool.

Meanwhile, gently heat the apricot jam with the water and brush a little over the top of the tart. Place the poached pears on top and brush with the remaining glaze. Decorate with whipped cream or finely chopped pistachio nuts.

Apple and Blackberry Amber

Serves 4-6

550g (¼ lb) cooking apples, peeled, cored and chopped	*1-2 tablespoons water*
2-4 tablespoons sugar	*2 eggs, separated*
grated rind and juice of ½ lemon	*100g (4 oz) blackberries, hulled*
	½ quantity Pâté Sucrée (see page 21)
25g (1 oz) butter	*50g (2 oz) castor sugar*

Place the apple, sugar, lemon rind and juice, butter and water in a saucepan. Cover and cook until the apple is a soft pulp. Remove from the heat, cool slightly then beat in the egg yolks. Fold in the blackberries.

Roll out the prepared pastry on a lightly-floured surface to a round large enough to line a 20–23-cm (8–9-inch) pie plate (see page 50). Use the pastry trimmings to make small pastry cut-out shapes. Dampen with water and secure these around the pastry rim.

Pour the apple and blackberry mixture into the dish and cook in a preheated moderate oven (180°C, 350°F, Gas Mark 4) for 20–25 minutes until the pastry is cooked and golden and the apple and blackberry mixture is set. Reduce the oven temperature to cool (150°C, 300°F, Gas Mark 2).

Whisk the egg whites until they stand in stiff peaks. Gradually whisk in all but 1 tablespoon of the castor sugar until the mixture is thick and glossy. Spoon or pipe the meringue over the apple and blackberry filling and dust with the remaining castor sugar. Cook for 30 minutes or until the meringue is golden and crisp. Serve hot with cream.

Apple and Raisin Flan

Serves 6

PASTRY
100g (4 oz) plain flour
pinch of salt
65g (2½ oz) butter
15g (½ oz) castor sugar
1 egg, separated
1 teaspoon cold water
FILLING
450g (1 lb) cooking apples,
  peeled, cored and sliced

25g (1 oz) butter
2 large (size 1, 2) eggs, beaten
50g (2 oz) light soft brown
  sugar
90ml (3 fl oz) single cream
grated rind of 1 lemon
100g (4 oz) raisins
icing sugar to dust

Prepare the pastry: sift the flour and salt into a mixing bowl. Cut the butter into small pieces and rub into the flour until the mixture resembles fine breadcrumbs. Stir in the sugar and egg yolk with the water and bind to a firm dough. Wrap in greaseproof paper or cling film and chill for 30 minutes.

Prepare the filling: cook the apples in the butter until very soft, about 20 minutes. Beat until the mixture forms a smooth purée. Allow to cool.

Roll out the pastry on a lightly-floured surface to a round large enough to line a 20-cm (8-inch) flan dish or ring set on a baking tray (see page 54). Bake 'blind' in a preheated moderately hot oven (200°C, 400°F, Gas Mark 6) for 10 minutes (see page 54). Remove the foil or beans. Beat the egg white lightly and use to brush the base and sides of the partially cooked pastry case. Return to the oven and cook for a further 5 minutes.

Mix the cooled apple purée with the eggs, sugar, single cream, lemon rind and raisins. Spoon into the pastry case. Reduce the oven temperature to 190°C, 375°F, Gas Mark 5 and cook for 45–50 minutes until golden. Serve warm or cold, dusted with icing sugar.

Yorkshire Curd Tarts

Makes 10

1 quantity Shortcrust Pastry
  (see page 12)
25g (1 oz) butter
25g (1 oz) castor sugar
100g (4 oz) cottage cheese,
  sieved

1 egg, beaten
grated rind and juice of 1
  lemon
4 teaspoons single cream
50g (2 oz) currants

Roll out the prepared pastry on a lightly-floured surface and cut out ten (7.5-cm/3-inch) rounds with a fluted scone or biscuit cutter. Fit into greased patty tins and chill while preparing the filling.

Cream the butter with the sugar until light and fluffy. Stir in the cheese, egg, lemon rind and juice, cream and currants, mixing well. Divide the filling evenly between the pastry cases.

Cook in a preheated moderately hot oven (200°C, 400°F, Gas Mark 6) for about 25 minutes until well-risen and cooked through. Allow to cool slightly before transferring to a wire rack to cool completely.

Honey-glazed Fruit Tart

Serves 6

PASTRY
175g (6 oz) plain flour
50g (2 oz) icing sugar
75g (3 oz) butter
3 egg yolks
2 drops vanilla essence
FILLING
150ml (¼ pint) double cream
100g (4 oz) cream cheese,
   softened
1 tablespoon icing sugar,
   sifted
6 oranges, peeled, pith
   removed and sliced into
   rounds
100g (4 oz) green grapes,
   seeded
4 tablespoons clear honey

Prepare the pastry: sift the flour and sugar into a mixing bowl. Cut the butter into small pieces and rub into the flour and sugar until the mixture resembles fine breadcrumbs. Beat the egg yolks with the vanilla essence and stir into the dry ingredients. Bind well with a round-bladed knife to a smooth dough. Wrap in polythene or cling film and chill for 20 minutes.

Roll out on a lightly-floured surface and use to line a 20-cm (8-inch) flan tin (see page 54). Prick the base well with a fork and bake 'blind' in a preheated hot oven (220°C, 425°F, Gas Mark 7) for 15 minutes (see page 54). Remove the foil or beans and bake for a further 5–6 minutes. Allow to cool.

Prepare the filling: whip the cream until it stands in soft peaks and fold into the softened cream cheese and icing sugar. Spread over the base of the cold pastry case. Arrange the orange slices and grapes in circles on the cream cheese.

Heat the honey in a small pan until bubbling and slightly thickened. Remove from the heat and brush over the fruit. Chill well before serving. Best eaten on day of making.

Ginger Treacle Tart

Serves 6

1 quantity Shortcrust Pastry
   (see page 12)
½ Jamaican ginger cake
100g (4 oz) mixed dried fruit
1 dessert apple, peeled, cored
   and grated

grated rind and juice of 1
   lemon
4 tablespoons golden syrup
2 tablespoons milk

Roll out the prepared pastry on a lightly-floured surface and use to line a 23-cm (9-inch) pie plate or shallow flan tin (see page 54). Reserve any pastry trimmings.

Coarsely grate the ginger cake and mix with the dried fruit, apple, lemon rind, lemon juice, golden syrup and milk. Spread over the pastry case to within 2.5 cm (1 inch) of the edges. Dampen the pastry rim with water. Roll out the pastry trimmings and cut into thin strips. Arrange in a criss-cross or lattice design over the filling (see page 94).

Place on a baking tray and cook in a preheated moderately hot oven (200°C, 400°F, Gas Mark 6) for about 35–40 minutes until the pastry is golden. Serve with fresh single, double or soured cream.

Festive Mincemeat Flan

Serves 8

PASTRY
225g (8 oz) plain flour
150g (5 oz) butter
1 tablespoon castor sugar
1 egg yolk
1-2 tablespoons cold water
milk to glaze
FILLING
½ Jamaican ginger cake

350g (12 oz) mincemeat
2 dessert apples, peeled, cored
   and chopped
100g (4 oz) green grapes,
   halved and seeded
grated rind and juice of 1
   orange
4 tablespoons brandy or apple
   juice

Prepare the pastry: sift the flour into a mixing bowl. Cut the butter into small pieces and rub into the flour until the mixture resembles fine breadcrumbs. Stir in the sugar and egg yolk and mix to a firm dough with the water. Roll out two-thirds of the pastry on a lightly-floured surface and use to line a 23-cm (9-inch) flan tin (see page 54). Chill for 15 minutes.

Prepare the filling: coarsely grate the ginger cake and mix with the mincemeat, apple, grapes, orange rind, orange juice and brandy or apple juice. Spoon into the pastry case. Roll out the remaining pastry thinly and stamp out about twelve to fourteen (7.5-cm/3-inch) rounds with a fluted cutter. Dampen the pastry case rim and arrange the rounds overlapping around the edge. Brush with milk to glaze and cook in a preheated moderately hot oven (200°C, 400°F, Gas Mark 6) for 35–40 minutes until golden. Serve hot or cold with cream or pouring custard.

Melon and Plum Plate Tart

Serves 4

1 quantity Pâte Sucrée
  (see page 21)
1 (552-g/1 lb 3-oz) can Victoria
  plums, drained
1 small melon, weighing about
  675g (1½ lb), skinned and
  cut into 2.5-cm (1-inch) cubes

2 tablespoons castor sugar
½ teaspoon ground ginger
beaten egg to glaze

Roll out the prepared pastry on a lightly-floured surface to a round 2.5 cm (1 inch) larger than a 20-cm (8-inch) pie plate or shallow pie dish. Place the plums and melon in the base of the dish and sprinkle with the sugar and ginger. Trim a 1-cm (½-inch) strip from the edge of the pastry and use to line the dampened rim of the dish. Dampen the pastry rim with water and cover with the lid (see page 50). Trim, seal and flute the edges. Use any pastry trimmings to decorate the pie as liked.

Brush with beaten egg to glaze and cook in a preheated moderately hot oven (200°C, 400°F, Gas Mark 6) for 25–30 minutes until the pastry is a rich golden brown.

Dust the tart with extra castor sugar if liked and serve hot or cold with whipped cream or custard.

Grape and Lemon Tart

Serves 6

1 quantity Nutmeg Pastry
  (see page 18)
2 tablespoons lemon curd
2 eggs
25g (1 oz) castor sugar
300ml (½ pint) milk

¼ teaspoon vanilla essence
TOPPING
6 black grapes
little egg white
15g (½ oz) castor sugar
3 slices lemon, halved

Roll out the prepared pastry on a lightly-floured surface and use to line a 20-cm (8-inch) flan ring set on a baking tray (see page 54).

Spread the lemon curd over the base of the pastry case. Beat the eggs with the castor sugar until well mixed. Place the milk and vanilla in a saucepan and heat until hand-hot. Pour over the eggs, mixing well. Strain the mixture into the pastry case. Cook in a preheated moderately hot oven (190°C, 375°F, Gas Mark 5) for 35–40 minutes until the pastry is golden and the custard has set. Allow to cool slightly then transfer to a serving plate.

Halve three of the grapes and remove the seeds. Remove the seeds from the remaining three whole grapes. Brush all the grapes with the egg white and toss in the sugar to coat. Leave the frosted grapes to dry. Decorate the edge of the tart with lemon slices and grape halves, and place the whole grapes in the centre. Serve slightly chilled.

SWEET PUDDINGS, PIES AND DESSERTS

Blackberry and Apple Pudding

Serves 4-6

*1 quantity Suet Crust Pastry
  (see page 38)
450g (1 lb) fresh or frozen
  blackberries, hulled
450g (1 lb) cooking apples,
  peeled, cored and sliced*

*225g (8 oz) sugar
2 tablespoons plain flour
custard or cream to serve*

Roll out the prepared pastry on a lightly-floured surface to a round about 5cm (2 inches) larger than the diameter of a 900-ml (1½-pint) pudding basin. Cut a quarter section from the pastry round and reserve for a lid (see page 67).

Lift the remaining piece of pastry and ease it into the basin, pinching the two cut edges together to seal and moulding the pastry onto the base and around the sides of the basin (see page 67).

Mix the blackberries with the apples, sugar and flour, tossing well to mix. Spoon into the pastry-lined pudding basin, packing down well. Roll out the remaining pastry to a round large enough to make a lid. Dampen the pastry edges with water and cover with the lid. Pinch the edges together firmly to seal. Cover with a piece of pleated foil and secure with string. Steam the pudding over a gentle heat for 2½–3 hours or until well-risen, spongy and cooked through, checking the water level regularly. Serve hot with custard or cream.

Apple Spiced Roll

Serves 4-6

*½ quantity Suet Crust Pastry
  (see page 38)
225g (8 oz) cooking apples,
  peeled, cored and chopped
50g (2 oz) demerara sugar*

*75g (3 oz) mixed dried fruit
½ teaspoon ground mixed
  spice
castor sugar to dredge*

Roll out the prepared pastry on a lightly-floured surface to a rectangle about 30 × 15cm (12 × 6 inches).

Mix the chopped apples with the sugar, dried fruit and spice. Spread onto the pastry rectangle leaving a 2.5 cm (1-inch) border around the pastry. Dampen the border with water and roll up like a Swiss roll to make a roly-poly (see page 63). Wrap in greased foil and steam over a moderate heat for 2 hours. Turn out and dredge with castor sugar. Slice the spiced roll and serve with custard or cream.

Cinnamon Banana Dumplings

Makes 12

¼ *quantity Puff Pastry (see*
  page 25)
3 large firm bananas
1 tablespoon lemon juice

75g (3 oz) granulated brown
  sugar
1 teaspoon ground cinnamon
beaten egg to glaze

Roll out the prepared pastry on a lightly-floured surface to a
rectangle 50 × 38cm (20 × 15 inches). Cut into twelve (13-cm/5-
inch) squares.

Cut the bananas into twelve equal pieces and toss in the
lemon juice. Place a banana piece in the centre of each pastry
square. Mix the sugar with the cinnamon and sprinkle a little
over each banana piece, reserving any sugar and cinnamon
mixture. Fold the dumplings into envelope shapes (see page 62),
securing the edges with a little beaten egg. Brush the whole
dumplings with beaten egg to glaze and dust with the
remaining cinnamon and sugar mixture.

Place on a greased baking tray and cook in a preheated hot
oven (220°C, 425°F, Gas Mark 7) for 15–20 minutes until the
pastry is puffed up and golden brown. Serve warm.

Apple Pockets

Serves 6

¼ *quantity Puff Pastry (see*
  page 25)
3 medium dessert or eating
  apples, peeled, cored and
  halved

1 egg, beaten
2 tablespoons icing sugar
3 tablespoons clear honey

Roll out the prepared pastry on a lightly-floured surface to a
rectangle 23 × 40cm (9 × 16 inches). Place the apple halves, cut
sides down on the pastry, allowing space between each.

Using a sharp knife, cut apple shapes with stalk and leaf
around the apple halves. Place on a dampened baking tray and
brush with the beaten egg. Cook in a preheated moderately hot
oven (200°C, 400°F, Gas Mark 6) for 20 minutes.

Remove from the oven and dust the apple pockets with icing
sugar. Return to the oven and cook for a further 5 minutes.
Serve hot, topped with the honey.

Profiteroles with Butterscotch Sauce

Serves 6

*1 quantity Choux Pastry (see
  page 34)*
300ml (½ pint) double cream
25g (1 oz) hazelnuts, chopped
BUTTERSCOTCH SAUCE
1 tablespoon cornflour

150ml (¼ pint) milk
25g (1 oz) unsalted butter
100g (4 oz) soft brown sugar
½ teaspoon vanilla essence

Spoon the prepared pastry in a piping bag fitted with a 1-cm (½-inch) plain nozzle and pipe about 30 small mounds of pastry onto greased baking trays (see page 73). Cook in a preheated hot oven (220°C, 425°F, Gas Mark 7) for 15–20 minutes until crisp, well-risen and golden. Pierce a small hole in the side of each profiterole to allow any steam to escape. Return to the oven and cook for a further 5 minutes. Allow to cool on a wire rack.

Whip the cream until it stands in soft peaks. Fold in the hazelnuts and use to fill the profiteroles.

Prepare the sauce: mix the cornflour to a smooth paste with a little of the milk. Place the remaining milk in a saucepan with the butter and sugar. Heat gently until the sugar dissolves. Add the cornflour paste and cook until the sauce thickens, stirring. Add the vanilla essence and cook for 2 minutes. Serve the sauce warm or cold over the filled profiteroles.

VARIATION

Profiteroles with chocolate sauce: Prepare and cook the profiteroles as above. To make the chocolate sauce, melt 125g (4½ oz) plain chocolate in a bowl over a saucepan of hot water. Boil 25g (1 oz) castor sugar with 450ml (¾ pint) water for 5 minutes then add, spoon by spoon, to the chocolate. Simmer for a further 10 minutes until the chocolate sauce coats the back of a spoon. Serve warm or cold over the filled profiteroles.

Sticky Raisin Roly-Poly

Serves 4

*finely grated rind and juice of
  1 lemon*
*1 quantity Light Suet Crust
  Pastry (see page 38)*
*25g (1 oz) fresh white
  breadcrumbs*

75g (3 oz) raisins
milk to glaze
200ml (7 fl oz) golden syrup

Knead the lemon rind into the prepared pastry or add with the dry ingredients prior to mixing. Roll out on a lightly-floured surface to a rectangle 25 × 30cm (10 × 12 inches). Sprinkle with the breadcrumbs and raisins to within 2cm (¾ inch) of the edges. Brush the edges with a little milk. Spoon over half of the golden syrup, spreading evenly. Turn in the edges on two long sides and one short side and brush again with milk. Roll up, from the short folded edge, like a Swiss roll. Wrap loosely in greased foil and place on a baking tray. Twist the ends of the foil to seal.

Cook in a preheated moderately hot oven (190°C, 375°F, Gas Mark 5) for 40 minutes. Meanwhile, place the remaining golden syrup in a pan with the lemon juice and heat to boiling. Allow to cool slightly.

Cut the roly-poly into thick slices with the lemon syrup sauce poured over. Serve with pouring custard.

Peach and Walnut Pie

Serves 6

1 quantity Walnut Pastry
  (see page 24)
6 large peaches, skinned and
  stoned

1 egg white, beaten
castor sugar to dust

Roll out two-thirds of the prepared pastry on a lightly-floured surface and use to line the base and sides of a 23-cm (9-inch) loose-bottomed flan tin (see page 54).

Cut the peaches into thick slices and arrange in the pastry case. Roll out the remaining pastry on a lightly-floured surface to a round large enough to make a lid. Dampen the pastry rim with water and cover with the lid. Trim, seal and flute the edges if liked. Make a small hole in the centre of the pie to allow any steam to escape during cooking. Use any pastry trimmings to decorate the pie as liked. Brush with egg white and dust with castor sugar.

Cook in a preheated moderately hot oven (200°C, 400°F, Gas Mark 6) for about 25–30 minutes until light golden and crisp. Serve with clotted cream, thickened cream or custard if liked.

Puff Apple and Date Strudel with Cinnamon Cream

Serves 6

675g (1½ lb) cooking apples,
peeled, cored and coarsely
chopped
2 tablespoons lemon juice
50g (2 oz) fresh white
breadcrumbs
50g (2 oz) demerara sugar
50g (2 oz) ground almonds
100g (4 oz) stoned dates,
coarsely chopped

½ quantity Puff Pastry (see
page 25)
milk to glaze
25g (1 oz) flaked almonds
1-2 tablespoons castor sugar
CINNAMON CREAM
300ml (½ pint) whipping
cream
2 teaspoons ground cinnamon

Mix the apple with the lemon juice, breadcrumbs, sugar, almonds and dates.

Roll out the prepared pastry on a lightly-floured surface to a rectangle about 50 × 30cm (20 × 12 inches). Spoon the apple mixture down the centre 10cm (4 inches) of the pastry, leaving a 4-cm (1½-inch) border at either end.

Brush the pastry with milk and fold the edges over the apple to completely enclose, sealing well. Place on a dampened baking tray, seam side down, in a semi-circular or horseshoe shape and brush with milk to glaze. Sprinkle with the almonds and castor sugar.

Cook in a preheated moderately hot oven (190°C, 375°F, Gas Mark 5) for 35–40 minutes until well-risen, golden brown and cooked through.

Meanwhile, prepare the cinnamon cream. Place the cream in a bowl with the cinnamon and whip until the cream stands in soft peaks. Chill before serving. Serve the strudel warm, cut into slices, with the chilled cinnamon cream.

Danish Apple and Raisin Pie

Serves 6

PASTRY
225g (8 oz) plain flour
pinch of salt
75g (3 oz) butter
100g (4 oz) Esrom cheese,
finely grated
1 egg yolk
2 tablespoons cold water

FILLING
675g (1½ lb) cooking apples,
peeled, cored and thickly
sliced
4 tablespoons granulated
sugar
50g (2 oz) raisins
beaten egg to glaze

180

Prepare the pastry: sift the flour and salt into a mixing bowl. Cut the butter into small pieces and rub into the flour until the mixture resembles fine breadcrumbs. Add the Esrom cheese, mixing well. Mix the egg yolk with the water and add to the dry ingredients. Bind to a firm but pliable dough. Wrap in greaseproof paper or cling film and chill for 30 minutes.

Divide the pastry in half. Roll out one half on a lightly-floured surface to a round large enough to line a 23-cm (9-inch) pie plate (see page 50).

Prepare the filling: place the apples in a saucepan with 1 tablespoon water, the sugar and raisins. Cover and simmer gently for 10 minutes. Allow to cool.

Pile the apple mixture onto the pastry base. Roll out the remaining pastry to make a lid. Dampen the pastry rim with water and cover with the lid. Trim, seal and flute the edges. Use any pastry trimmings to decorate the pie as liked.

Brush with beaten egg to glaze and cook in a preheated moderately hot oven (200°C, 400°F, Gas Mark 6) for 20–30 minutes until the pastry is golden brown and cooked through. Serve hot or cold with cream.

St Clement's Mince Pies

Makes about 18

1 quantity Orange or Lemon
  Shortcrust Pastry (see
  page 13)
225g (8 oz) mincemeat
1 tablespoon brandy or
  curaçao
grated rind of 1 small orange
icing sugar to dust

Roll out two-thirds of the prepared pastry on a lightly-floured surface and cut out about eighteen rounds using a 7.5-cm (3-inch) fluted biscuit or scone cutter. Carefully fit into greased tartlet tins (see page 58). Blend the mincemeat with the brandy or curaçao and orange rind and spoon equal amounts into the pastry cases.

Gather the remaining pastry and trimmings together and roll out on a lightly-floured surface. Using a small star-shaped cutter, stamp out about eighteen star-shaped pieces of pastry. Place on top of the filled tartlets and cook in a preheated moderately hot oven (200°C, 400°F, Gas Mark 6) for 20–25 minutes until golden and cooked through. Transfer to a wire rack and allow to cool. Serve warm, dusted with a little icing sugar.

Double-crust Apple Pie

Serves 6–8

PASTRY
275g (10 oz) plain flour
pinch of salt
65g (2½ oz) lard
65g (2½ oz) butter or
 margarine
3–4 tablespoons iced water

FILLING
900g (2 lb) cooking apples,
 peeled, cored and sliced
100g (4 oz) soft light brown
 sugar
2 tablespoons cornflour
milk or beaten egg to glaze
castor sugar to dust

Prepare the pastry: sift the flour and salt into a mixing bowl. Cut the lard and butter or margarine into small pieces and rub into the flour until the mixture resembles fine breadcrumbs. Add the water and bind to a firm but pliable dough.

Divide the pastry in half. Roll out one half on a lightly-floured surface to a round large enough to line a greased 25-cm (10-inch) pie plate (see page 50).

Prepare the filling: place the apples in a bowl and toss with the sugar and cornflour. Pack into the pastry case. Roll out the remaining pastry to make a lid. Dampen the pastry rim with water or beaten egg and cover with the lid. Trim, seal and flute the edges. Use any pastry trimmings to decorate the pie as liked. Make a small hole in the top of the pie for any steam to escape. Brush with milk or beaten egg to glaze and dust with castor sugar.

Place on a baking tray and cook in a preheated hot oven (220°C, 425°F, Gas Mark 7) for 30–40 minutes until well-risen, golden brown and cooked through. Serve hot or cold with whipped cream.

VARIATIONS
Double-crust rhubarb and ginger pie: Prepare and cook as above but use 900g (2 lb) sliced rhubarb and 15g (½ oz) chopped preserved ginger instead of the apples.
Double-crust plum and orange pie: Prepare and cook as above but use 900g (2 lb) halved and stoned plums with the grated rind of 1 orange instead of the apples.
Double-crust apricot and raspberry pie: Prepare and cook as above but use 450g (1 lb) peeled, halved and stoned apricots and 350g (12 oz) hulled raspberries instead of the apples.
Double-crust gooseberry and orange pie: Prepare and cook as above but use 900g (2 lb) topped and tailed gooseberries with the grated rind of 1 orange instead of the apples.
Double-crust cherry and lemon pie: Prepare and cook as above but use 900g (2 lb) stoned sweet cherries with the grated rind of 1 lemon instead of the apples.

Apple Meringue Pie

Serves 6

1 quantity Plain or Lemon
  Shortcrust Pastry (see
  page 12)
675g (1½ lb) cooking apples,
  peeled, cored and thickly
  sliced
100g (4 oz) golden granulated
  sugar
25g (1 oz) butter

grated rind and juice of
  ½ lemon
MERINGUE
4 egg whites
225g (8 oz) golden granulated
  sugar

Roll out the prepared pastry on a lightly-floured surface and use to line a 24-cm (9½-inch) flan tin (see page 54). Bake 'blind' in a preheated moderately hot oven (200°C, 400°F, Gas Mark 6) for 15 minutes (see page 54). Remove the foil or beans and cook for a further 5 minutes.

Meanwhile, place the apples in a saucepan with the sugar, butter, lemon rind and juice. Stew the apples until very soft. Purée through a fine sieve. Allow to cool slightly then pour into the pastry case.

To make the meringue, whisk the egg whites until they stand in stiff peaks. Whisk in half of the sugar until thick and glossy. Fold in the remaining sugar. Spoon or pipe decoratively over the apple filling and cook for 10–15 minutes until the meringue is a light golden colour. Serve hot or cold, cut into wedges.

American Sweet Vinegar Pie

Serves 6

PASTRY
250g (9 oz) wheatmeal flour
1 teaspoon salt
65g (2½ oz) butter or
  margarine
65g (2½ oz) lard
4 tablespoons cold water
FILLING
25g (1 oz) wheatmeal flour
pinch of salt
1 teaspoon ground mixed spice

4 egg yolks
175g (6 oz) soft light brown
  sugar
200ml (7 fl oz) soured cream
3 tablespoons cider vinegar
200g (7 oz) raisins or
  sultanas
2 egg whites
SPICED CREAM
150ml (¼ pint) double cream
1 teaspoon ground mixed spice

Prepare the pastry: place the flour and salt into a mixing bowl. Cut the butter or margarine and lard into small pieces and rub into the flour until the mixture resembles fine breadcrumbs. Add the water and bind to a stiff but manageable dough. Wrap in greaseproof paper or cling film and chill for 15 minutes.

Roll out on a lightly-floured surface to a round large enough to line a 25-cm (10-inch) flan tin (see page 54).

Prepare the filling: mix the flour with the salt and mixed spice. Whisk the egg yolks with the sugar until very light and thick, about 10 minutes. Fold in the flour mixture with the soured cream, vinegar and raisins or sultanas. Whisk the egg whites until they stand in stiff peaks. Fold into the soured cream mixture. Pour into the pastry case and cook in a preheated hot oven (230°C, 450°F, Gas Mark 8) for 10 minutes.

Reduce the oven temperature to moderate (180°C, 350°F, Gas Mark 4) and cook for a further 20 minutes until golden brown and firm to the touch.

Meanwhile whip the cream with the mixed spice until it stands in soft peaks. Serve the pie warm, cut into thick wedges and topped with the spiced cream.

CAKES, GÂTEAUX AND CHEESECAKES

Eccles Cakes

Makes 12

50g (2 oz) butter
2 tablespoons castor sugar
1 egg yolk
finely grated rind of 1 lemon
½ teaspoon ground mixed spice
½ teaspoon ground nutmeg
150g (5 oz) currants

25g (1 oz) chopped mixed
  candied peel
1 quantity Flaky Pastry (see
  page 32)
milk to glaze
castor sugar to sprinkle

Beat the butter with the sugar until light and fluffy. Beat in the egg yolk, lemon rind, mixed spice and nutmeg. Fold in the currants and mixed peel, mixing well.

Roll out the prepared pastry on a lightly-floured surface and cut out twelve (10-cm/4-inch) rounds. Place an equal quantity of fruit mixture on each round. Dampen the pastry edges with water and, with the fingertips, draw up the edges of each round so that they meet in the centre, completely enclosing the filling. Press well together to seal. Turn each cake over and flatten slightly with a rolling pin. Make three slits in the top of each with a sharp knife.

Place on dampened baking trays and brush with milk to glaze. Sprinkle generously with castor sugar and cook in a preheated hot oven (220°C, 425°F, Gas Mark 7) for 15–20 minutes or until well risen and golden brown. Allow to cool on a wire rack.

Puff Pastry Baklavas

Makes 8

75g (3 oz) almonds, finely
  chopped
75g (3 oz) walnuts, finely
  chopped
½ teaspoon ground cinnamon
½ teaspoon ground mixed spice

150ml (¼ pint) clear honey
½ quantity Puff Pastry (see
  page 25)
20g (¾ oz) butter, melted
juice of ½ lemon

Mix the almonds with the walnuts, cinnamon, mixed spice and 50ml (2 fl oz) of the honey.

Roll out the prepared pastry on a lightly-floured surface to a 33-cm (13-inch) square. Cut into four equal squares. Place one square of pastry in a shallow 16.5-cm (6½-inch) square cake tin lined with foil. Brush with a little melted butter. Cover with another square of pastry and the nut and honey filling. Cover

186

with a third square of pastry, brush with butter and top with the remaining pastry square. Brush again with butter and, using a sharp knife, cut through the top two layers of pastry to form four equal squares. Cut each square again diagonally, as before, to form eight triangles. Cook in a preheated moderately hot oven (200°C, 400°F, Gas Mark 6) for 25 minutes until well-risen and golden brown.

Meanwhile prepare the baklava syrup. Mix the lemon juice with the remaining honey and make up to 150ml (¼ pint) with water. Bring to the boil and cook for 2 minutes.

Slowly strain the hot syrup over the cooked baklava, still in its tin, and leave to soak for 2 hours. Cut through the bottom two layers of pastry with a sharp knife to make eight puff pastry baklavas to serve.

Raspberry Mille Feuilles

Serves 4-6

½ quantity Puff Pastry (see page 25)
4 tablespoons raspberry jam
1 tablespoon kirsch or orange juice
300ml (½ pint) double cream

2 teaspoons castor sugar
350g (12 oz) raspberries, hulled
75g (3 oz) icing sugar
few whole raspberries to decorate

Roll out the prepared pastry on a lightly-floured surface to a rectangle about 20 × 25cm (8 × 10 inches). Cut into three rectangles lengthwise and place on a dampened baking tray. Cook in a preheated hot oven (220°C, 425°F, Gas Mark 7) for 20 minutes until well risen and golden brown. Allow to cool on a wire rack.

Using a sharp knife, trim the rectangles to the same size, crushing any trimmings to be used later (see page 69). Mix the jam with the kirsch or orange juice. Whip the cream with the castor sugar until it stands in soft peaks. Place one pastry strip on a serving dish. Top with half of the jam and cream. Top with half of the raspberries and another strip of pastry. Cover with the remaining jam and cream. Top with the remaining raspberries and final piece of pastry.

Mix the sifted icing sugar with a little water to make a thick glacé icing and spread over the top piece of pastry. Sprinkle a border of crushed crumbs around the icing. Decorate with a few whole raspberries. Chill lightly to serve.

Gâteau Pithiviers

Serves 6

*½ quantity Puff Pastry (see
  page 25)
100g (4 oz) ground almonds
100g (4 oz) castor sugar
40g (1½ oz) unsalted butter,
  melted*

*2 egg yolks
2 tablespoons double cream
2 tablespoons dark rum
beaten egg to glaze
1 tablespoon icing sugar,
  sifted*

Roll out the prepared pastry on a lightly-floured surface and cut out two (23-cm/9-inch) rounds. Line a 20-cm (8-inch) pie plate with one of the rounds.

Cream together the almonds, sugar, butter, egg yolks, cream and rum. Spoon into the pastry case. Dampen the pastry rim with water and cover with the remaining pastry round. Press the edges firmly to seal. Using a sharp knife make about twelve cuts around the edge of the gâteau. Using your fingers, push up the pastry at each cut to form petal shapes.

Brush with beaten egg to glaze and cook in a preheated hot oven (230°C, 450°F, Gas Mark 8) for 10-15 minutes. Reduce the oven temperature to moderately hot (200°C, 400°F, Gas Mark 6) and cook for a further 20–30 minutes until golden and cooked through.

Dust with the icing sugar and place under a preheated hot grill to caramelise the sugar. Serve the gâteau warm with single cream or yogurt.

Hazelnut and Raspberry Galette

Serves 6

*GALETTE
175g (6 oz) butter
100g (4 oz) castor sugar
grated rind of ½ lemon
175g (6 oz) plain flour
100g (4 oz) hazelnuts, skins
  removed and roughly
  chopped*

*FILLING
300ml (½ pint) whipping
  cream
1 tablespoon icing sugar, sifted
675g (1½ lb) raspberries,
  hulled*

Prepare the galette: cream the butter and sugar together until light and fluffy. Beat in the lemon rind and fold in the sifted flour. Knead until the dough is smooth and chill for 30 minutes.

Divide the pastry into three. Roll out each portion on a lightly-floured surface to an 18-cm (7-inch) round. Pinch the edges of the rounds to form a decorative trim. Place on greased baking trays and sprinkle the top of each with the nuts. Cook in a preheated moderate oven (180°C, 350°F, Gas Mark 4) for 20–25 minutes until golden. Allow to cool slightly on the trays then transfer to a wire rack to cool completely.

Prepare the filling: whip the cream with the icing sugar until it stands in soft peaks. Mix 450g (1 lb) of the raspberries with two-thirds of the cream. Use to sandwich the rounds together. Pipe the remaining cream in swirls on top of the galette and decorate with the remaining raspberries. Chill for 30 minutes before serving.

VARIATION

Hazelnut and Strawberry galette:

Prepare and cook as above but use 675g (1½ lb) strawberries instead of the raspberries.

Peach and Pineapple Meringue Shortbread

Serves 4-5

SHORTBREAD
225g (8 oz) plain flour
50g (2 oz) castor sugar
175g (6 oz) butter
FILLING
1 (410-g/14¼oz) can sliced peaches, drained

1 (227-g/8-oz) can pineapple pieces, drained
MERINGUE
2 large (size 1,2) egg whites
100g (4 oz) castor sugar

Prepare the shortbread: mix the flour with the sugar in a bowl. Cut the butter into small pieces and rub into the flour and sugar until the mixture resembles moist breadcrumbs. Knead together to make a smooth, firm dough.

Turn out onto a lightly-floured surface and knead until smooth and free from cracks. Roll out to a round large enough to fit into the base of a 20-cm (8-inch) flan ring set on a baking tray (see page 54). Press down gently and prick the base well with a fork. Cook in a preheated cool oven (150°C, 300°F, Gas Mark 2) for 50–60 minutes until firm and light golden brown. Allow to cool on the baking tray.

When cool, arrange the peach slices overlapping around the edges of the shortbread and pile the pineapple pieces in the centre, reserving two pieces for decoration.

Whisk the egg whites until they stand in stiff peaks. Whisk in half of the sugar until smooth and glossy then fold in the remainder. Pile the meringue on top of the pineapple, leaving the edges of the peaches showing.

Increase the oven temperature to moderately hot (190°C, 375°F, Gas Mark 5) and cook the shortbread for 15–20 minutes until the meringue is golden brown. Serve warm or cold, decorated with the reserved pineapple pieces.

189

Deep Dish German Apple Cake

Serves 8

PASTRY
150g (5 oz) self-raising flour
150g (5 oz) butter
65g (2½ oz) sugar
1 small (size 6) egg, lightly
* beaten*

FILLING
900g (2 lb) dessert apples,
* peeled, cored and sliced*
lemon juice
castor sugar
ground cinnamon

Prepare the pastry: sift the flour into a mixing bowl. Cut the butter into small pieces and rub into the flour until the mixture resembles fine breadcrumbs. Stir in the sugar, mixing well. Blend in the egg and bind to a loose dough. Chill for 30 minutes.

Press the pastry with the fingertips into a greased 23-cm (9-inch) deep loose-bottomed flan tin. Toss the apples in the lemon juice and layer neatly in the pastry case, sprinkling with sugar and cinnamon between each layer.

Cook in a preheated moderately hot oven (190°C, 375°F, Gas Mark 5) for 50 minutes. Allow to cool in the tin before unmoulding. Serve cut into wedges and topped with whipped cream.

Apple Strudel

Serves 6

½ quantity Phyllo or Strudel
* Pastry (see page 41)*
450g (1 lb) cooking apples,
* peeled, cored and sliced*
50g (2 oz) raisins
50g (2 oz) sultanas

1 teaspoon ground cinnamon
3 tablespoons toasted
* breadcrumbs*
25g (1 oz) butter, melted
icing sugar to dust

Stretch the prepared pastry to a large paper-thin sheet on a lightly-floured cloth (see page 43).

Mix the apple with the raisins, sultanas, cinnamon and 1 tablespoon of the breadcrumbs. Brush the pastry with a little of the melted butter and sprinkle with the remaining breadcrumbs. Top with the fruit mixture, spreading evenly. Roll up into a long roll. Place on a greased baking tray and shape into a horseshoe. Brush with the remaining butter and cook in a preheated moderately hot oven (200°C, 400°F, Gas Mark 6) for 20-25 minutes until golden. Dust with sifted icing sugar and serve warm, cut into thick slices.

Coffee and Hazelnut Pastry Cake

Serves 6–8

1 quantity Galette Pastry (see page 23)
225g (8 oz) unsalted butter, softened
225g (8 oz) icing sugar
2 tablespoons strong black coffee

150ml (¼ pint) double cream
75g (3 oz) hazelnuts, coarsely chopped
whipped cream and whole hazelnuts to decorate

Divide the prepared pastry into three. Roll out each piece on a lightly-floured surface to a 23-cm (9-inch) round and place on greased baking trays. Prick well with a fork and cook in a preheated moderate oven (180°C, 350°F, Gas Mark 4) for 15 minutes. Allow to cool slightly then transfer to a wire rack to cool completely.

Meanwhile, beat the butter with the sifted icing sugar until light and fluffy then beat in the coffee. Whip the cream until it stands in soft peaks and fold in half of the hazelnuts.

To assemble the cake, place one pastry round on a serving plate. Reserve one quarter of the coffee buttercream and divide the remainder into two equal portions. Spread one portion over the pastry round. Cover with half of the hazelnut mixture. Top with a second pastry round. Cover with the second portion of coffee buttercream and the remaining hazelnut mixture. Finally top with the remaining pastry round.

Coat the sides of the cake with the reserved coffee buttercream spreading evenly, then coat the sides of the cake with the remaining hazelnuts.

To decorate the cake, pipe swirls of whipped cream around the top edge of the cake. Decorate with whole hazelnuts and dust with sifted icing sugar. Chill for 2 hours before serving, cut into wedges.

Creamy Raisin Cheesecake

Serves 6–8

PASTRY
50g (2 oz) self-raising flour
50g (2 oz) castor sugar
50g (2 oz) margarine
1 egg, beaten
FILLING
450g (1 lb) curd cheese

75g (3 oz) castor sugar
grated rind of 1 lemon
1 tablespoon plain flour
3 eggs, beaten
150ml (¼ pint) double cream
¼ teaspoon vanilla essence
40g (1½ oz) raisins

Prepare the pastry: mix the flour with the sugar in a mixing bowl. Cut the margarine into small pieces and rub into the flour and sugar until the mixture resembles fine breadcrumbs. Stir in the egg, mixing well. Spread evenly over the base of a greased 18-cm (7-inch) loose-bottomed spring form tin. Cook in a preheated moderate oven (160°C, 325°F, Gas Mark 3) for 20–25 minutes. Allow to cool slightly.

Prepare the filling: beat the curd cheese with the sugar and lemon rind until light and fluffy. Fold in the flour and beat in the eggs, a little at a time. Whisk in the double cream and vanilla essence and finally fold in the raisins. Pour onto the pastry base and cook in the oven for 1–1½ hours until the filling is set and firm. Turn off the oven heat and leave the cheesecake to cool in the oven with the door ajar for about 2 hours. Chill before serving, cut into thick wedges.

Blackberry Cheesecake

Serves 6

1 quantity Shortcrust
  Pastry (see page 12)
FILLING
275g (10 oz) cottage cheese,
  sieved
2 large (size 1,2) eggs, beaten
300ml (½ pint) soured cream
5 tablespoons castor sugar

1 tablespoon lemon juice
1 teaspoon vanilla essence
pinch of salt
TOPPING
225g (8 oz) frozen blackberries
3 tablespoons sugar
1 teaspoon cornflour
2 teaspoons kirsch

Roll out the prepared pastry on a lightly-floured surface to a round large enough to line a 20-cm (8-inch) flan tin (see page 54). Bake blind in a preheated moderately hot oven (200°C, 400°F, Gas Mark 6) for 15–20 minutes (see page 54). Remove the foil or beans.

Prepare the filling: whisk the cottage cheese with the eggs, soured cream, sugar, lemon juice, vanilla essence and salt until smooth. Pour into the partially cooked pastry case. Reduce the oven temperature to moderately hot (190°C, 375°F, Gas Mark 5) and cook the cheesecake for 45 minutes or until set. Allow to cool.

Prepare the topping: cook the blackberries and sugar over a low heat until tender. Remove the berries with a slotted spoon or sieve and reserve. Reduce the juice over a high heat to 150ml (¼ pint). Add the cornflour and kirsch and cook, stirring constantly, until clear and thickened. Allow to cool then stir in the cooked berries. When cold spoon on top of the cheesecake and chill thoroughly. Cut into wedges to serve.

Italian Cheesecake

Serves 6-8

1 quantity Pâte Sucrée (see page 21)
1.25kg (2½ lb) ricotta cheese, sieved
100g (4 oz) castor sugar
2 tablespoons plain flour
¼ teaspoon salt
½ teaspoon vanilla essence grated rind of 1 orange

grated rind and juice of 2 lemons
4 egg yolks
3 tablespoons raisins
2 tablespoons chopped mixed candied peel
2 tablespoons slivered almonds
1 egg white, lightly beaten

Divide the prepared pastry in half. Roll out one half on a lightly-floured surface to a 23-cm (9-inch) round. Use to line the base of a greased 23-cm (9-inch) spring form tin (see page 60). Prick well with a fork and cook in a preheated moderately hot oven (200°C, 400°F, Gas Mark 6) for 10 minutes.

Roll out the remaining pastry into one strip long enough to line the sides of the tin. Grease the edges of the tin and place the pastry strip round, moulding it gently onto the base to seal (see page 50). Reserve any pastry trimmings.

Beat the ricotta with the sugar, flour, salt, vanilla essence, grated orange and lemon rind, lemon juice and egg yolks until well blended. Stir in the raisins and mixed peel. Pour into the pastry case and level the surface. Sprinkle with the almonds. Roll out the pastry trimmings and cut into thin strips. Position on top of the cheesecake in a lattice design (see page 94). Brush the strips lightly with the egg white.

Reduce the oven temperature to moderate (180°C, 350°F, Gas Mark 4) and cook the cheesecake for 45-55 minutes or until the crust is golden brown and the filling is firm to the touch. Allow to cool slightly then remove the spring sides. Still on its metal base, allow the cheesecake to cool on a wire rack. Cut into wedges to serve.

Walnut and Cheesecake Squares

Makes 16

PASTRY
*150g (5 oz) soft light brown
  sugar*
175g (6 oz) plain flour
*75g (3 oz) walnuts, coarsely
  chopped*
75g (3 oz) butter, melted
FILLING
*225g (8 oz) full-fat cream
  cheese*

100g (4 oz) castor sugar
1 egg, beaten
1 tablespoon lemon juice
2 tablespoons milk
grated rind of ½ lemon

Prepare the pastry: mix the sugar with the flour in a mixing bowl. Add the walnuts and toss to coat. Add the butter and mix with the fingertips until the mixture resembles coarse breadcrumbs. Sprinkle two-thirds of this mixture on the base of a 20-cm (8-inch) shallow square cake tin. Cook in a preheated moderate oven (180°C, 350°F, Gas Mark 4) for 15 minutes.

Prepare the filling: place the cream cheese, sugar and egg in a bowl. Whisk the mixture until smooth and creamy. Fold in the lemon juice, milk and lemon rind, mixing well. Spoon the cheesecake mixture over the baked pastry base and level with a spatula. Sprinkle the remaining biscuit mixture over the filling. Cook the cheesecake for a further 25 minutes. Allow to cool in the tin before cutting into sixteen (5-cm/2-inch) squares. Remove the squares carefully with a spatula to serve.

SMALL SWEET PASTRIES AND BISCUITS

Cinnamon and Mincemeat Crunchaways

Makes 16

PASTRY
225g (8 oz) plain flour
2 teaspoons cream of tartar
1 teaspoon bicarbonate of soda
½ teaspoon ground cinnamon
pinch of salt

100g (4 oz) butter
100g (4 oz) castor sugar
1 egg, beaten
FILLING
225g (8 oz) mincemeat
3 tablespoons flaked almonds

Prepare the pastry: sift the flour with the cream of tartar, bicarbonate of soda, cinnamon and salt into a mixing bowl. Cut the butter into small pieces and rub into the flour until the mixture resembles fine breadcrumbs. Add the sugar and mix to a soft dough with the egg.

Roll out on a well-floured surface or between sheets of non-stick paper and cut out sixteen (7.5-cm/3-inch) rounds and sixteen (6-cm/2½-inch) rounds. Fit the larger rounds into greased patty tins. Divide the mincemeat between the pastry cases and top with the smaller pastry rounds. (There is no need to dampen the edges of the pastry as the tops and bottoms will seal together during cooking.)

Sprinkle evenly with the flaked almonds and cook in a preheated moderately hot oven (200°C, 400°F, Gas Mark 6) for about 15 minutes. Allow to cool slightly in the tins before removing to a wire rack to cool completely.

Chocolate Éclairs

Makes 12

1 quantity Choux Pastry (see
  page 34)
300ml (½ pint) confectioner's
  custard or double cream,
  whipped

225g (8 oz) plain dessert
  chocolate, melted

Spoon the prepared pastry into a piping bag fitted with a 1-cm (½-inch) plain nozzle. Cover a buttered baking tray with greaseproof paper and pipe the pastry into 12 strips, about 9cm (3½ inches) long. Cut off each length with a knife, allowing about 4cm (1½ inches) between each strip for expansion (see page 72).

Cook in a preheated moderately hot oven (200°C, 400°F, Gas Mark 6) for about 15 minutes. Reduce the oven temperature a little to 190°C, 375°F, Gas Mark 5 and cook for a further 10–15 minutes until well-risen, firm and golden. Pierce the ends of each éclair with a knife to allow any steam to escape. Return to the oven for a further 5 minutes to dry out. Allow to cool on a wire rack.

When the éclairs are cold, cut a lid from each one and fill with the cold confectioner's custard or whipped cream. Spread the melted chocolate over the éclairs with a palette knife. Leave to set. Serve slightly chilled.

VARIATIONS

Coffee éclairs: Prepare, cook and fill the éclairs as above but coat with coffee glacé icing made by mixing 225g (8 oz) sifted icing sugar with 2 teaspoons instant coffee powder dissolved in 2 tablespoons hot water.

Lemon cream éclairs: Prepare and cook the éclairs as above but fill with a lemon cream mixture made by mixing 150ml (¼ pint) whipped double cream with 225g (8 oz) lemon curd. Coat with the chocolate as above.

Creamy Coffee Choux Puffs

Makes 12

*1 quantity Choux Pastry (see
 page 34)*
beaten egg to glaze
FILLING
300ml (½ pint) double cream
*1-2 tablespoons liquid coffee
 essence*

ICING
*1 teaspoon instant coffee
 granules or powder*
3 tablespoons hot water
25g (1 oz) castor sugar
175g (6 oz) icing sugar

Spoon the prepared pastry into a piping bag fitted with a 1-cm (½-inch) plain nozzle. Pipe small mounds of the mixture onto greased baking trays, allowing plenty of space between each for expansion (see page 73).

Brush lightly with beaten egg to glaze and cook in a preheated hot oven (220°C, 425°F, Gas Mark 7) for 20 minutes. Pierce a small hole at the side of each puff to allow any steam to escape. Return to the oven for a further 5 minutes. Allow to cool on a wire rack.

Whip the cream with the coffee until it stands in soft peaks. Split the choux puffs in half and fill with the coffee cream.

Prepare the icing: place the coffee, water and castor sugar in a pan and heat until the sugar dissolves. Remove from the heat and gradually add the sifted icing sugar, mixing well to make a smooth icing. Spoon a little over each bun and leave to set.

Quick and Easy Ring Doughnuts

Makes 20

225g (8 oz) plain flour
½ teaspoon bicarbonate of soda
1 teaspoon cream of tartar
pinch of ground cinnamon
25g (1 oz) butter

50g (2 oz) castor sugar
1 egg, beaten
milk if required
oil for deep frying
icing or castor sugar to dust

Sift the flour, bicarbonate of soda, cream of tartar and cinnamon into a mixing bowl. Rub in the butter until the mixture resembles fine breadcrumbs. Stir in the sugar, blending well. Add the egg and mix to make a stiff dough. Add a little milk if the dough is too dry and stiff.

Turn onto a lightly-floured surface and knead lightly until smooth and free from cracks. Roll out to about 1cm (½ inch) thickness. Cut out rings with a doughnut cutter or by using a large and small pastry cutter.

Heat the oil to 182°C (360°F) and add the doughnuts, a few at a time. Deep fry until golden brown, turning occasionally with a spatula or spoon. Drain with a slotted spoon and place on absorbent kitchen towel. Cook the remaining doughnuts the same way. Serve while still warm, dusted in sugar.

Sesame Cookies

Makes 36

100g (4 oz) sesame seeds
100g (4 oz) plain flour
¼ teaspoon bicarbonate of soda
100g (4 oz) butter or margarine

100g (4 oz) castor sugar
1½ tablespoons set honey
1 egg, beaten

Mix the sesame seeds with the flour and bicarbonate of soda. Cream the butter with the sugar until light and fluffy. Beat in the honey and egg with the dry ingredients, mixing to a stiff dough.

Turn onto a lightly-floured surface and roll into a long sausage shape about 4cm (1½ inches) thick. Wrap in foil and chill for at least 30 minutes.

Cut the pastry into 5mm (¼ inch) slices and place about 2.5cm (1 inch) apart, on greased baking trays. Cook in a preheated moderate oven (180°C, 350°F, Gas Mark 4) for 15 minutes until golden. Allow to cool on a wire rack. Store in an airtight container.

Raspberry and Cream Horns

Makes 10

¼ quantity Puff Pastry (see
   page 25)
beaten egg to glaze
100g (4 oz) raspberries, hulled

150ml (¼ pint) double cream
1 tablespoon icing sugar
1 teaspoon kirsch (optional)
icing sugar to dust

Roll out the prepared pastry on a lightly-floured surface and cut into about ten strips each measuring 1 × 35cm (½ × 14 inches). Dampen one edge of each pastry strip with water and carefully wind around a pastry horn mould (see page 68).

Place on a dampened baking tray and brush with beaten egg to glaze. Cook in a preheated hot oven (220°C, 425°F, Gas Mark 7) for 25 minutes until golden and cooked. Slip the horns from their moulds about 3-4 minutes from the end of the cooking time and return to the oven to dry out. Allow to cool on a wire rack.

Lightly crush about three-quarters of the raspberries. Whip the cream with the sifted icing sugar and kirsch, if used, until it stands in soft peaks. Fold in the crushed raspberries and use to fill the pastry horns. Decorate with the reserved raspberries and dust with sifted icing sugar. Chill lightly before serving.

Honeyed Oatmeal Biscuits

Makes 24

25g (1 oz) plain flour
225g (8 oz) oatmeal
pinch of salt

50g (2 oz) butter
1 tablespoon set honey

Mix the flour with the oatmeal and salt. Rub in the butter to form a coarse paste and bind to a firm dough with the honey. Place the pastry on a sheet of floured greaseproof paper. Cover with another piece of greaseproof paper and roll out very thinly. Remove the top piece of paper and cut the pastry into twenty-four rounds using a 5-cm (2-inch) scone or biscuit cutter.

Place the rounds on greased baking trays and cook in a preheated moderate oven (180°C, 350°F, Gas Mark 4) for 8-10 minutes until crisp and lightly browned. Allow to cool on the baking trays. Store in an airtight container.

Christmas Wreaths

Makes 24

1 quantity Almond Pastry (see
 page 24)
beaten egg white to glaze

2 tablespoons castor sugar
50g (2 oz) coloured glacé
 cherries, chopped

Take heaped teaspoons of the prepared pastry and shape into Christmas wreaths (see page 81). Place on greased baking trays and brush with beaten egg white to glaze. Sprinkle with the sugar and decorate with pieces of chopped coloured glacé cherries.

Cook in a preheated moderately hot oven (200°C, 400°F, Gas Mark 6) for 10–12 minutes. Allow to cool on a wire rack.

Easter Biscuits

Makes about 15

225g (8 oz) plain flour
½ teaspoon ground cinnamon
100g (4 oz) butter, softened
100g (4 oz) castor sugar
1 large (size 1,2) egg, beaten
grated rind of 1 lemon

50g (2 oz) currants
1 teaspoon milk
lightly beaten egg white to
 glaze
castor sugar to dust

Sift the flour and cinnamon into a bowl. Cream the butter and castor sugar until light and fluffy. Add the egg, a little at a time, beating well. Stir in the lemon rind. Work in the currants and cinnamon flour mixture with the milk to make a stiff dough.

Turn onto a lightly-floured surface and knead lightly until smooth and free from cracks. Roll out until about 5mm (¼ inch) thick. Cut out about fifteen rounds with a 7.5-cm (3-inch) fluted biscuit or scone cutter. Place on greased baking trays and prick with a fork. Brush with a little beaten egg white to glaze and dust lightly with sugar.

Cook in a preheated moderate oven (180°C, 350°F, Gas Mark 4) for 20 minutes until golden. Allow to cool on a wire rack. Will store in an airtight container for about 3–4 days.

Lemon Crunchies

Makes about 40

225g (8 oz) plain flour
1 teaspoon baking powder
100g (4 oz) butter
175g (6 oz) castor sugar

finely grated rind of 1 lemon
1 egg, beaten
1 teaspoon lemon juice
sugared lemon slices to decorate

Sift the flour and baking powder into a mixing bowl. Cut the butter into small pieces and rub into the flour until the mixture resembles fine breadcrumbs. Stir in the sugar and lemon rind. Mix to a fairly stiff dough with the egg and lemon juice.

Turn onto a lightly-floured surface and knead lightly until smooth and free from cracks. Divide the pastry in half and roll each into a 'sausage' shape about 30cm (12 inches) long. Wrap each roll in foil and chill for 4-6 hours.

Cut each roll into about twenty slices and place, cut side down, on lightly-greased baking trays, allowing a little space between each for spreading. Cook in a preheated moderately hot oven (190°C, 375°F, Gas Mark5) for 10-12 minutes until pale golden in colour. Cool a little then remove with a palette knife and allow to cool on a wire rack. Top each biscuit with a sugared lemon slice.

INDEX

204